Thank You Saint Jude

By

John Wallace Spencer

PHILLIPS PUBLISHING COMPANY
P.O. BOX 439
AGAWAM, MA 01001

ISBN 0-941219-01-1

Nihil Obstat:

Lector Deputatus:

Reverend Augustine P. Hennessy, C.P.

Imprimatur

Joseph F. Maquire, D.D.

Bishop of Springfield, Massachusetts

March 5, 1986

TABLE OF CONTENTS

THANK YOU SAINT JUDE

PRINTING HISTORY

1st printing September 1986
2nd printing November 1986
3rd printing April 1987
4th printing December 1987
5th printing October 1988

Phillips Publishing Company
P.O. Box 439
Agawam, MA 01001

Telephone (413) 789-2420

ISBN 0-941219-01-1

PRINTED IN THE UNITED STATES OF AMERICA

PREFACE

More than a decade of years ago, Doctor Karl Menninger wrote a book entitled; "Whatever Became of Sin?"

Today, more so than ever, almost any senior missionary belonging to an apostolic preaching community might well ask a similar question: "Whatever became of popular devotions?" There was a time when shrine churches all over this country drew crowds of the faithful who waited in long lines outside the church doors hoping to move into the next scheduled devotion.

It may have been in honor of Our Lady of Perpetual Help; a novena in honor of St. Jude; regular Monday devotions in honor of St. Paul of the Cross and St. Gabriel of the Most Sorrowful Virgin; or weekly devotions in honor of the Immaculate Conception of Mary, patroness of the Miraculous Medal.

Economic depressions, war-time fears, tensions, worries, life threatening epidemics, and other such disquieting situations have always called forth the rediscovery of popular devotion.

When people at large are free from an overhanging fear, devotion tends to remain a subsurface reality.

But, devotion is a much more profound reality than a provocative power luring devotees into churches with overflow crowds of prayerful clients.

Devotion is at the heart of all worshipful praise of God. It is an internal dynamic giving power and warmth to all acts of religion.

Still more, devotion is that interior yearning of the spirit which made Jesus Himself long to cast the fire of love upon this earth, and feel within Himself an eagerness to see it burst into flame.

In writing this carefully researched book on devotion to St. Jude, John Wallace Spencer has produced a work which is unmistakably a labor of love.

His own zeal in behalf of the honor due to the saintly apostle has led him to travel extensively throughout this country to visit St. Jude shrines.

The author has listened carefully to real-life stories of men and women who gave fascinating accounts of the impact St. Jude has made upon their interior life of grace and their pursuit of serenity of mind and heart.

Mr. Spencer knows how to tell a story. His interviews with clients of St. Jude have evoked self-revelation which is always edifying and, at times, imbued with gripping interest.

The story of how the "City of St. Jude" in Montgomery, Alabama was founded by Passionist, Father Harold Purcell was especially meaningful to me.

This same great priest of vision was also the founding editor of Sign Magazine which was published by the Passionists and had a life-span of nearly sixty years.

"Thank You St. Jude" is marked with an enthusiasm which empowers the author's initiative to impart useful information about works of devotion which many good people are not well-informed.

The author brings to his work a gentle effort at imparting a catechesis; he instructs his readers without being heavy-handed or patronizing.

John Wallace Spencer has given us a work of piety which is a testimony of his own devotion to St. Jude.

s/ Father Augustine P. Hennessy, C.P., S.T.D.

....

FATHER AUGUSTINE PAUL HENNESSY

Father Augustine Paul Hennessy, C.P., preacher, journalist, and theologian has been a Passionist since August 15, 1934 and was ordained to the priesthood by Bishop Cushing in the Boston Cathedral on May 1, 1941.

His Community (Passionist Order, or the Congregation of the Discalced Clerks of the Most Holy Cross and Passion of our Lord Jesus Christ) was founded in 1720, by (St.) Paul of the Cross (1694-1775).

The Passionist Order, which practices strict poverty, grew rapidly and now has missionaries working in 53 countries; on every continent.

Father Augustine served as the associate editor of "Sign" magazine from 1945 until 1948. In January 1967 he returned to the magazine as the editor and continued in that capacity until 1975.

In the interim, (1970), Father Augustine Paul was one of twenty-five theologians from the United States and Canada who were invited and participated in the World Congress in Brussels.

Presently, Father Augustine Paul resides at Our Lady of Sorrows Monastery in West Springfield, Massachusetts. In addition to his love of writing, he is much sought after by local parishes throughout the northeast to conduct novenas and missions.

However, the working Passionist is primarily engaged in preaching parish renewals and retreats, especially to priests, monks, friars, nuns, and lay persons who have taken religious vows.

INTRODUCTION

This work began during a casual conversation between the author and an acquaintance.

During the informal exchange of words and ideas, the author offhandedly mentioned that Jude Thaddeus was his patron saint.

With obvious interest, the man picked up on the remark. He explained how he had noticed paid *Thank You Saint Jude* ads in several different publications, and wanted to know more.

Thereafter, whenever the two men met the conversation always worked its way around to the "Patron Saint of Difficult and Hopeless Cases."

Unable to provide all the answers for the barrage of questions, the author decided to purchase a book about his patron saint.

Several large religious articles stores were contacted without success. Apparently, no books about Saint Jude Thaddeus were in print.

Determined to learn more, the author turned to the reference departments of a couple of main city libraries.

Other than a few insignificant bits of information, no books, reports or in depth studies had been published about St. Jude Thaddeus.

As a devotee and author, his assignment was unmistakable; to research and write a detailed portrait-biography of the "Patron Saint of the Desperate."

It was to be an informative and entertaining study, with a few fascinating stories about people who had been helped through St. Jude's intercession.

Now that the research and writing is complete, it must be understood that this book is not a scientific report. For to have taken on such a project would have involved getting entangled in historical disputes over unimportant details.

All of the presented stories and incidents encompassing the; *life, missionary adventures, and devotees* of Saint Jude Thaddeus are supported by carefully selected sources, or first person interviews.

This work has not been targeted to any specific faith, but was written for all who want to know more about a very special friend.

If it's true that through understanding comes love, then this work cannot help but draw St. Jude's faithful earthly friends even closer to him.

Yet, of greater importance, there is now, for the first time, an entertaining reference book through which strangers can be introduced to the "The Patron Saint of Hopeless and Desperate Cases."

CHAPTER I

NEVER SAY CAN'T

There are many definitions of *faith,* but the most concise was written nearly two thousand years ago by St. Paul in his letter to the Hebrews *(11:1-40).*

> *"...Faith is that which gives substance to our hopes, which convinces us of things we cannot see..."*

People speak of having *faith* in: families, the administration of justice, oneself, political parties, United States currency, *(In God We Trust),* The Almighty, St. Jude, and so on.

Knowing by faith is another way of saying; "I truly believe and accept an idea, or belief in spite of all arguments in opposition."

Faith can be *positive* or *negative.* For instance, atheists have negative faith because they believe that a supreme being *does not* exist.

Debating God or the intercessory power of St. Jude with those of *negative* faith is wasted effort. As the saying goes:

> *"To those who have positive religious faith, no explanation is necessary. To those with negative faith, no explanation is possible."*

Ironically, when issues of religious belief are debated by the two sides, based solely on *faith,* each is certain their point of view is correct.

It's common for disagreements of faith to occur between people who have the same basic belief. *Christianity is a perfect example with its hundreds of offshoots.*

To understand a person without religious faith is difficult because belief in a higher authority is the first sign of civilization. There has never been found a society without some form of *faith* in a supreme being.

Scholars generally agree that the foundation of religious faith begins when one person in a primitive society recognizes the perfect order of the universe, earth, seasons, birth, life and death.

Since the theme of the opening chapter is *faith,* it's appropriate to begin with a story about a man who has publicly demonstrated unquestioning faith in God and in the intercessory power of St. Jude.

As happens to so many of us, our subject found himself at a critical crossroad in life. In desperation he prayed through St. Jude to help him make the right decision in solving his seemingly hopeless situation.

The person who is the topic of our story was born in Deerfield, Michigan on *January 6, 1914* and named, *"Amos Joseph Muzyad Alphonsus Jacobs" (pronounced Yahoob).*

Amos was the fifth of *9* children of Charles and Margaret Christian *(Simon)* Jacobs, a deeply religious Catholic couple who had immigrated to the United States from Lebanon. When Amos was a baby his family moved to Toledo, Ohio.

Mr. Jacobs, a poorly paid laborer, could only afford a rundown, small apartment over a pool hall for his young growing family.

At the height of the roaring twenties, *10* year old Amos got a job at the Columbia Burlesque Theater selling candy and soda from aisle to aisle *(candy butcher)*.

A couple of nights a week the young boy worked until about two-thirty in the morning.

Even though Amos walked home alone through the empty streets of the sleeping city, his mother wasn't unduly worried for his safety because she had strong religious *faith*. With the birth of each of her children, Mrs. Jacobs placed them under the protection of St. Mary.

Testimony to the depth of the woman's *faith* was demonstrated when Amos' brother Danny was only a few months old.

While the baby was asleep a rat jumped into his crib in a vicious attack. The bites were very severe and the boy went into convulsions.

Doctors at the hospital informed Mrs. Jacobs that her son was in critical condition and probably would not survive the night.

Refusing to accept the grim prognosis she prayed to St. Mary, promising that if her son's life was spared, for a full year she'd beg pennies for the poor.

With each passing day Danny grew stronger and the doctors were amazed at the boy's rapid recovery.

Amos' mother was a woman of her word and despite the fact that the Jacobs family was among the poorest in Toledo, every day she went from door to door begging pennies for other poor families.

Throughout Amos' formative teenage years he continued working at the burlesque theater. Unlike most children his age, he knew exactly what he wanted to do with his life.

He enjoyed his job for it gave him the opportunity to study the styles of the top comedians. More than anything, he wanted to be an entertainer.

Soon he began picking up a few odd jobs singing, and telling jokes at banquets and other local functions.

When Amos was *15* years old, the Great Depression of *1929* struck, and survival for his family became very difficult. A few months later, armed with nine years of education, the star struck boy dropped out of Woodward High School in quest of a show business career.

It only took a couple of weeks for the budding entertainer to realize he couldn't earn enough money to meet the barest of necessities. With youthful enthusiasm, Amos decided to patiently await his show business break.

> *Between infrequent engagements, he held a variety of jobs including; night watchman, drill press operator's assistant, busboy, and semi-professional basketball player.*

It took until *1934* before Amos landed his first solid show business engagement as master of ceremonies of a popular Detroit radio program, the *Happy Hour Club.* That's when he met, and fell in love with Rose Marie Cassaniti, a singer on the show.

When the radio contract expired, Amos was offered a master of ceremonies position at *Bert's Beer Garden* also in Detroit. It was there that he picked up his first small, but faithful following.

Amos and Rose Marie got married on *January 15, 1936.* During the next four years the determined young entertainer enjoyed a measure of success working in dozens of saloons. His act included doing impressions, telling jokes and singing.

In the meantime, *(1938)*, Rose Marie gave birth to their first daughter, Margaret *(Marlo Thomas, wife of Phil Donahue)*.

In the *'30's* and early *'40's* show business was a poorly paid occupation and frequently the young family didn't have enough money to make ends meet.

During the summer of *1940*, Amos was performing as the master of ceremonies of the *Club Morocco* in Detroit. Even though he only earned a few dollars a night, he was happy because it was a steady engagement.

Without warning Amos' world suddenly fell apart. One night shortly after the staff arrived, the owners announced that in two weeks the club would close its doors forever.

Amos felt fear because he didn't have any prospects for another show business job. For the first time in his *26* year life, the struggling entertainer experienced hopelessness.

A few nights later a loyal fan entered the club. Seeing the lines of worry furrowed across Amos' face, the man tried to cheer him up with idle conversation.

Suddenly the mood changed and the man became serious. He started telling Amos an amazing story about his wife who had had terminal cancer.

He described how he had knelt on the cold marble floor of the hospital waiting room throughout the entire night before his wife was to undergo surgery for removal of a cancerous tumor.

Over and over he repeated the same prayer to St. Jude. It was late morning before the surgeon came to the waiting room to report on the outcome of the operation.

The doctor stated he was confused because the operation revealed the woman's malignant tumor had somehow mysteriously vanished overnight.

The man then handed Amos a card with a picture of St. Jude Thaddeus on one side and a prayer printed on the other.

Briefly he explained that when the "Patron Saint of Hopeless Cases" does a favor, that person must thank him publicly by doing something in return.

The next morning Amos and Rose Marie talked about his less than successful show business career.

She suggested that perhaps it might be wise if he left the entertainment field for something with a steady paycheck; the grocery business or possibly sales.

Several evenings later, on the way to the club, Amos was cold and discouraged. He entered the chapel of St. Peter and St. Paul to think and get warm.

After sitting in the peaceful church for some time, he took the St. Jude card out of his wallet, and recited the printed prayer. It was then he made this vow:

> *"Help me find my place in life and I will build you a shrine where the poor, the helpless and the hopeless may come for comfort and aid."*

Several days later the club closed. With all their possessions packed into an old beat-up Buick, Amos, Rose Marie, and Margaret Julia set out for his parent's home.

The plan was a long shot. Rose Marie was to stay in Toledo with Amos' family while he made one last attempt to make it in show business.

PRAYER CARD DISCIPLES

It's astonishing how many devotees began their friendship with St. Jude through a prayer card, or booklet carrying disciple.

This is accomplished by a massive unorganized force of self-appointed missionaries who travel around spreading the word about the intercessory power of the "Patron of the Desperate."

Dedicated members are constantly on the alert for friends, or strangers who might be experiencing a troubled time. Once identified, the ambassadors seize the opportunity to introduce the person to St. Jude by the gift of a free prayer card or booklet.

Missionaries are required to explain the conditions which go along with every little printed message of hope. Recipients should be instructed that after Saint Jude helps them resolve their problems through his intercession, they become obligated to publicly express appreciation.

Fulfillment of the commitment can be accomplished in many ways including placing "Thank You St. Jude" ads in publications or by becoming a prayer card carrying disciple.

Although the pledge is treated as a sanctioned tradition, there's neither historical evidence establishing its foundation, nor any documentation supporting the custom.

Nonetheless, the pyramid style missionary approach has been extremely effective. At nearly any gathering the mere mention of St. Jude's name will surely produce several little printed messages of hope for all to see.

After a couple of days at home, Amos headed east toward Cleveland where he had a few show business connections.

Alone on the highway, his thoughts raced from one subject to another. Suddenly he was overpowered by the feeling he was heading in the wrong direction.

The entertainer can't explain what it was, except he knew he should be driving westward.to Chicago.

Without understanding or reason he turned the old car around and pointed it toward the windy city.

Soon after his arrival, Amos' show business career caught hold. One good radio job led to another. Before long Amos Jacobs was a successful and very busy radio character actor.

With money no longer a problem, Amos wanted to branch out into stand-up comedy; in a real nightclub.

Checking around, he found out there was an opening for a stand-up comic at the *5100 Club,* a cheap Chicago nightspot which had been an automobile showroom.

The audition was a snap and Amos easily got the engagement. However, he was ashamed of the grubby atmosphere and worried that if word got around he was working in such a sleezy joint his growing reputation would be damaged.

As a safeguard, he decided it would be best to change his stage name. On opening night, using his youngest and oldest brothers' first names, with only a handful of customers in the club, *"Danny Thomas"* walked out on stage.

He was an instantaneous smash hit and news about the funny unknown comedian spread all over Chicago.

Within a few months it was "SRO" *(standing room only)* with crowds waiting in long lines to catch his act. Over the months, as Danny Thomas drew one capacity audience after another, his salary went from *$50 to $500* a week.

It's the kind of story movies are made from, except it actually happened. The happy entertainer was atop a show business rocket streaking toward stardom.

Success didn't spoil or change Danny and he kept faith with his religion. Throughout the passing years, nearly every morning on the way home from the *5100 Club,* he'd stop in at St. Clement's Church for the five o'clock Mass.

One morning after the services, he was relaxing in the peaceful church atmosphere when he noticed a little pamphlet on the pew.

Picking it up, he was surprised to see it was a novena booklet from the *National Shrine of St. Jude* right there in Chicago. At that moment he remembered his promise.

> *Danny is sure the pamphlet was his patron saint's way of giving him a gentle reminder. Never again did he forget his vow to build a shrine for St. Jude.*

But, the popular entertainer was in demand, and free time was at a premium. Moreover, he couldn't decide on the kind of shrine to build, or what form it should take.

Once he thought about constructing a clinic in some remote primitive jungle community. Rose Marie suggested a large statue, or a side altar in a church, but nothing seemed right.

Months slipped into years. By *1943*, full of confidence, Danny was ready to take on the big time nightspots of New York City.

Moving from the midwest was difficult because he loved the people and the feelings were mutual. Nevertheless, the Thomas family moved east.

Danny's first big time engagement was at the famous *La Martinique* nightclub.

When a group of his Chicago fans found out about his premier opening, they chartered a bus to New York City.

As Danny walked out on stage and saw the familiar faces in the audience, he felt at home and the opening night jitters disappeared.

While playing New York's *Roxy Theater*, in 1943, Rose Marie gave birth to their second daughter, Theresa *(Terry)* Cecelia.

Danny had an uncanny creative ability which sometimes even surprised him. For instance take the night he was booked on *The Fanny Brice Show,* one of the nation's most popular weekly network radio programs.

Needing a funny new character, Danny came up with *Jerry Dingle* whose shenanigans served him well for many shows.

The next year, Danny volunteered to go with Marlene Dietrich's USO *(United Service Organization)* unit to entertain American soldiers fighting the war in Europe.

Later, he formed his own USO entertainment troupe which he took to the men and women serving in the Pacific.

When World War II ended, Danny returned to Chicago for a successful lengthy engagement at the *Chez Paree* nightclub.

In a single decade Danny Thomas had gained considerable nationwide popularity as a standup entertainer. Yet, he was constantly searching for a different show business experience.

Nobody was surprised when he decided to try his talents at motion picture acting. Without thought of failure, Danny moved his family, now two daughters and a son, Charles *(Tony)* Anthony, to Beverly Hills, California.

Danny Thomas' first motion picture was released in the fall of *1947* with four more to be completed within the next five years.

In between films he toured the nightclub and theater circuit appearing at several top show business spots including *Ciro's* in Hollywood and the *London Palladium* in England.

The new up-and-coming medium of television caught Danny's interest and at every opportunity he'd appear on the tube.

Danny Thomas was on just about all of the important network television shows including the two most popular; *All-Star Review* and *The Colgate Comedy Hour.*

Nearly a dozen years raced by since Danny had been reminded about his promise to St. Jude. Still, there were no firm plans for a shrine.

That is until the night Danny had a horrifying nightmare. It was about a young boy who had been seriously injured in an accident.

The child was rushed to the hospital by ambulance, however, after arrival nobody attended to the boy wounds and the youngster bled to death.

Shaken by the vivid nightmare, Danny kept associating the dream with the fan who had given him the St. Jude prayer card in Detroit years earlier.

His thoughts went back to the promise his mother had made to St. Mary when his younger brother was at the threshold of death.

Slowly, out of the confusion an idea for a St. Jude shrine began taking form. Danny started thinking in terms of a hospital. Not just an ordinary hospital, but a special research center where children with *incurable* diseases could come to be helped.

To determine if the public would financially support such a gigantic venture, Danny organized a fund-raising benefit.

As a test, he used the audience who attended the *1951* midwest premiere of his picture *"I'll See You in My Dreams"*.

After the showing, Danny went up on the stage and told the audience about his idea and asked for their contributions.

Any doubts he had about building a children's research hospital as St. Jude's shrine were gone, as the audience pledged *$51,000*.

For the next two years, the money collected was held in escrow while Danny busily made movies, appeared on television shows, and performed coast to coast in one nightclub after another.

By *1952*, Danny had enough of traveling and wanted to devote more time to his growing family.

He explained to a producer-friend that he wanted a good television script and asked if he'd keep a lookout for a plot that would fit his style of comedy.

This gave the producer an idea which developed into a situation comedy about an entertainer who wanted to get off the road to spend more time with his family.

In *1953*, ABC-TV aired the first episode of *Make Room for Daddy* starring Danny Thomas.

For *18* years the comedian had been living out of a suitcase, packing and unpacking in hotel room after hotel room. Now he had more free time than he knew what to do with.

When Danny announced he was going back on the road to launch a fund raising campaign for the St. Jude hospital shrine, Rose Marie wasn't the least bit surprised.

His first stop was Indianapolis to meet and win the backing of *Mike Tamer* a successful restaurateur. The two men hit it off, and set up a working relationship for the development of the *St. Jude Children's Research Hospital* project.

Mike assumed duties as business advisor, while Danny devoted his talents to public relations and fund-raising. They established ALSAC *(American Lebanese Syrian Associated Charities)* the central fund-raising organization for the hospital project.

From *1957 to 1971,* Indianapolis served as the center of operations, as well as headquarters of the national executives' offices. In fact Indy was being *seriously considered as the site for the St. Jude Children's Research Hospital.*

Danny was concerned the Catholic Church might object to his using St. Jude's name for a nondenominational project. To find out, he presented his plans to the *Archbishop of Chicago, Samuel Cardinal Stritch.*

Danny explained how he wanted to build a private institution to serve physically underprivileged children of all faiths, and races.

The hospital would not have a cash register or an accounts receivable *(billing)* department because no charges would be made for care regardless of the parent's ability to pay.

The Archbishop throught the project was a wonderful idea. However, he suggested that before making a final decision on Indianapolis, Danny should look to Memphis, Tennessee.

He pointed out that the southern city had an exceptionally fine medical community, and the *University of Tennessee's Medical School* had a reputation as being one of the best in the nation.

With Danny's permission, Archbishop Stritch introduced him to several important Memphis business and government leaders who expressed an eager willingness to give their full support to the enormous undertaking.

Everything pointed to the largest city in Tennessee as the perfect location. Danny and Mike discussed the advantages and disadvantages, and agreed St. Jude's hospital should be constructed in Memphis.

With selection of the location fixed, Danny directed his attention to the monumental task of raising the necessary building funds.

Mrs. Jacobs *(Danny's mother)* had always said, *"talk is cheap."* So, to get the project underway, Danny contributed a quarter of a million dollars of his own money.

He took his fund raising campaign nationwide with scores of benefit performances. Like it or not Danny Thomas was again packing and unpacking his suitcases.

The comedian spoke to any group who'd listen . He made personal appearances, twisted friends' arms, and persuaded show business associates to donate their money and time.

Through his tireless efforts, in *November 1958,* just off Highway *51* in Memphis, Tennessee, the site for St. Jude's hospital was officially dedicated. At that moment Danny realized the enormity of the undertaking. It was only the beginning, a tremendous amount of money still had to be raised.

As Mrs. Jacobs had done so many years earlier, her son was out begging from Catholics, Protestants, Jews, Moslems, and particularly from those of his own heritage through ALSAC.

Gathering donations for St. Jude's hospital from people of various religious faiths wasn't difficult. Most people understood that Danny Thomas' hospital was to be a nonsectarian medical facility.

Its only connection to Christianity would be the name and a ten-foot tall white marble statue of St. Jude which Danny purchased in Rome and had shipped to Memphis.

It took an entire decade to raise the necessary capital. On *February 4, 1962,* twenty-two years after Amos Jacobs made his promise, the *St. Jude Children's Research Hospital* was officially dedicated with admission of the first child for treatment.

When the speeches were over, and the well-wishers had left, Danny proudly walked out the front door of the children's research facility. As he passed the statue of St. Jude, he looked up at the "Patron Saint of the Desperate and the Hopeless," and gestured toward the building as if to say, *"there it is."*

At that moment Danny Thomas believed his obligation had been fulfilled. However, like so many others, he soon realized that nobody ever quits St. Jude.

EPILOGUE

As of this writing, Danny Thomas has dedicated his life to the *St. Jude Children's Research Hospital*.

He continually makes speeches, personal appearances and convinces friends and associates to do the same.

If Danny has learned anything about St. Jude, it is that the powerful saint can never be outdone.

He often explains; *"Whatever you do in the name of St. Jude, is always returned a thousand times over."*

As a guest on the *Johnny Carson show*, Danny told the story of being interviewed on another television talk program.

He said that part way through the interview the host asked his producer how much time was left.

As a joke Danny replied, "According to my *Timex*, it's ten eighteen."

A few days later, a *$10,000* check arrived from the Timex Corporation with an enclosed letter thanking him for the unsolicited commercial.

He revealed, *"I get found money like that all the time. All I do is endorse the checks over to St. Jude's hospital."*

The relationship of St. Jude and Danny Thomas has caused people to think of the famous multi-millionaire magnate of the entertainment industry as a kind of living saint.

Whenever the subject of his piety is brought up, Danny quickly sets the record straight:

"As for organized religion, I go to Mass on Sundays and Holy Days and that's about it. I'm just a man who has tremendous faith in God and St. Jude."

Thanks to this man of faith, in the little more than two decades since the research facility opened in *1962,* the number of patient rooms have more than doubled. A seven story addition was completed in *1975,* and another new building went up in *1981.*

In terms of numbers of patients and treatment successes, St Jude's has become the largest children's cancer research center in the world.

As of this writing, patients have been accepted from *39* states and *29* foreign countries. Care is provided for more than *2,000* children with cancer. Additional programs for youngsters with certain other catastrophic diseases and illnesses are also provided.

Although the hospital accepts insurance benefits when available, the question of whether a family has insurance is never a consideration of a patient's admission. Not a single child as ever been refused acceptance at St. Jude's because of an inability to pay.

Through his persuasive talents, the dedicated entertainer remains the hospital's chief fund raiser. By spreading his message of devotion to St. Jude, Danny Thomas is also the saint's unofficial chief public relations director.

Danny's long-range goal for St. Jude's hospital is to gather *$300-million* in trusts to ensure perpetual funding of the research facility. This guarantees money would always be available for human resources, research, maintenance, and replacement of the facilities, equipment, and property.

In simplified terms, the interest generated by the trusts, would assure that all the money ever needed to cover the hospital's operating expenses will be provided without ever using the principal sum.

Understandably Danny will not be able to personally gather such a staggering amount of money during his lifetime. However, he has faith that through the generosity of the millions of St. Jude devotees, the perpetual financial goal will be realized.

For the address and information about tax-deductible gifts, contributions, bequests and legacies, see Appendix D.

The idea for the title of this chapter came from one of Danny's favorite poems, written by Edgar A. Guest.

CAN'T

Can't is a word that is foe to ambition
An enemy ambush to shatter your will
Its prey is forever a man with a mission
And bows but to courage and patience and skill
So hate it with hatred that's deep and undying
For once it is welcomed 'twill break any man
And whatever the goal you are seeking, keep trying
And answer this demon by saying, I can.

MYSTERIOUS COINCIDENCE OF NUMBER 51

An interesting coincidence is how the number *51* periodically turned up during Danny Thomas' life. His first important show business engagement was at the *5100 Club*. The first fund raising drive for St. Jude's hospital took place in *1951;* the amount of money pledged totalled *$51,000*. St. Jude's Children's Research Hospital was constructed on *Highway 51*.

PARTIAL MOTION PICTURE AND TV RESUME

1947   First film - "The Unfinished Dance."

1948   "The Big City."

1949   "Call Me Mister."

1951   First starring role as Gus Kahn in "I'll See You In My Dreams."

1952   "The Jazz Singer."

1953-1957   "Make Room for Daddy" *(ABC-TV)* Star ring Danny Thomas, Marjorie Lord, Sherry Jackson, Rusty Hammer, and Angela Cartwright.

1957-1964   "Danny formed his own production company "Materto Productions," which produced: "The Danny Thomas Show" - "The Real McCoys" - "The Bill Dana Show."

1957-1964   "The Danny Thomas Show" (same as *Make Room for Daddy)* moved to CBS-TV. Soon it was rated among the top ten with a weekly audience of over 40-million viewers. For this Danny recieved the title of *"America's Favorite TV Comedian."*

1963   Cameo role - film, "Looking For Love."

1964-1968   Danny formed a production company with Sheldon Leonard, *"Thomas-Leonard Productions"* which was responsible for: "The Danny Thomas Show" - "The Andy Griffith Show" - and several spin-offs.

During this four year period Danny starred in several television specials, and made scores of guest star appearances.

1965   Cameo role, film - "Don't Worry We'll Think of a Title."

1967-1968   "The Danny Thomas Hour" *(NBC-TV)*, a 60-minute variety show featuring music, comedy and dramas. Danny appeared in every production.

1970-? Formed a producing partnership with Aaron Spelling "Thomas-Spelling Productions." The company turned out: "Mod Squad" - "The Guns of Will Sonnett" - "Rango" - "The New People" - "Chopper One."

1971-1972 "Make Room for Grandaddy" *(ABC-TV)*, an updated version of the sitcom, "Make Room For Daddy."

1972-1973 Starred in two NBC-TV specials.

1974 Voice only, movie - "Journey Back to Oz."

1976-1977 "The Practice" An NBC-TV situation comedy in which Danny played an aging doctor.

CHAPTER II

PUBLICATION PROMISED

Danny Thomas believes that *faith, prayer, and hard work* is the combination needed to convert *hopes, needs, and dreams* into reality.

The entertainer is convinced his meteoric rise in show business was in direct response to his prayers through St. Jude.

He sees the favor to be of such great value, that he's repaid St. Jude with a grand shrine and a lifetime of dedicated service.

Like young Amos Jacobs every person has experienced the feeling of overwhelming desperation.

Everyday, thousands of pieces of mail pour into St. Jude shrines from troubled people suffering with seemingly hopeless situations.

Within each bundle of mail are notes pleading for; *relief of pain, recovery from paralysis, blindness, heart disease, AIDS, and other crippling ailments and diseases where all medical knowledge has been exhausted.*

By and large, the vast majority of the mail comes from men, women, and children who are up against life's daily difficulties. The writers ask their patron saint for help with: *family problems, wayward children, sickness, injury, death, and the like.*

No personal problem is too insignificant.or too great for St. Jude. He's called on to break such habits and cravings as; *nail biting, dieting, cigarette and marijuana smoking, excessive drinking, etc.*

LETTERS REQUESTING INTERCESSORY PRAYER

"Please Pray to St. Jude for my husband who is very sick and cannot seem to accept his illness. He is mean to his teenage children and to me. Please pray my son can bear this treatment. I'm afraid it will get to him.

"Also, please pray for financial help, we need it badly, My nerves have had it. Name Withheld."

• • • • • • • • • •

"My problem is my teenage daughter who had always been such a good girl, that is, until lately. I don't know what's happened to her. She's been lying to me, staying out with boys (all night) and things like that.

"We always went to church every Sunday morning, but lately she tells me that when she turns to God, He turns His back on her. I guess she means we're poor.

"I'm all alone, raising four children; ages 21, 20, my troublesome daughter 18, and my youngest, 10, who isn't healthy and needs sunshine.

"My oldest two are working hard to get enough money so we can move to a dry climate.

"The day before yesterday, my daughter left the house, and I haven't seen or heard from her since. All I can beg is please, pray for me and my family. Signed Mrs. G. R."

• • • • • • • • • •

"I'm appealing for prayers to St. Jude for my son who suffers with a split personality and needs a cure which his doctors and psychologists are unable to provide.

"He's tried to kill us with a gun, sword, and hatchet. We escaped and ran for our lives. He's now in a mental hosptial, but can't stand being in there and cries for help to get out. My heart is breaking. Signed Mrs. H. F., Florida."

• • • • • • • • • •

"I'm making novenas to St. Jude that my fiance will find a job, we find a place to live, and have a smooth wedding. Signed Ms. M. G., Toronto"

• • • • • • • • • •

"St. Jude prayers are asked for my sister-in-law who has arthritis in her neck and arms and suffers terribly. His prayers are especially needed so she can resist the terrible depression that assails her. Signed Mrs. J.S.N., Pa."

•••••••••

"I beg St. Jude's prayers for my teenage son who is schizophrenic (emotionally distressed). He is locked up in a treatment center for trying to burn some houses, and still says he will start more fires if he gets out.

"We have been constantly involved with police and lawyers over our son. St. Jude's help is desperately needed. Signed Anonymous."

•••••••••

"I ask St. Jude's prayers for an 18 year old neighborhood boy whose divorced mother died recently, and his father is nowhere to be found.

"He has started running with the wrong crowd and is definitely on drugs.

"Now that he's all alone, he needs help more than ever. I'm not related, not even a friend, but at the funeral he was alone; nobody was caring for him. My heart goes out to this boy in desperate need of St. Jude's help. Signed D.F."

•••••••••

"I have made several novenas to St. Jude to please intercede for a healing for me. Among many other illnesses, I am legally blind, and am losing my hair. Singed Mr. J. K., Chicago."

•••••••••

"Please pray for my son and daughter-in-law, who are having marital problems, that they may soon get back together again; and that my son will return to the sacraments. Signed K.D.D."

•••••••••

"Some time ago my sister delivered my niece, stillborn. The same tragic ending came with her second pregnancy; at five months, she went into spontaneous labor which could not be stopped.

"Please pray for my sister, and her family. They need their Faith to remain strong now. Signed L.F."

•••••••••

"Here's my problem; pigeons! Pigeons up in the eaves, over my kitchen windows, over the back door, and walk; there's three generations of them. I have to use the walk at my own risk.

"The landlady has done repairs, but nothing about the pigeons. I really do ask prayers for what is "not" a funny situation. Signed Anonymous."

Others plead with the "Patron of the Desperate" for aid in finding; jobs, *mates, companions, lost articles, missing relatives, pets, and a lengthy list of other desires, wants and needs.*

The difference between a *favor* being granted, and an absolute *miracle* is often misunderstood. For example, Danny Thomas was granted a great *favor;* not a *miracle.*

Some devotees believe all answered prayers, no matter how insignificant are *miracles.* Holding the opposite view are those who see *miracles* in terms of bolts of lightning, complete with the thundering voice of God.

Whether *miracle, or favor* it's not always easy to recognize when prayers have been answered, for *God works in mysterious ways.*

People are so busy with their daily lives most never realize they've been guided, sometimes forced into situations which resulted in petitions being granted.

It takes the special gifts of *wisdom and insight* before a person is able to recognize how people, places, and things were subtly manipulated to bring about desired results.

Those holding *negative religious views* are blind to the sequence of events which lead the faithful to the solution of a desperate or seemingly hopeless situation.

With absolute conviction, *nonbelievers* readily explain every happening, which made the favor possible, as nothing more than simple coincidence.

Another factor clouding the recognition of answered prayers is that God doesn't always respond instantly. Some theologians suggest that perhaps the reason for delays is because the Lord knows when we're best able to handle particular situations, and holds off until the proper moment.

The wait between a call for help, and the response all too often leads to irritated impatience. Even St. Jude who is noted for urgent, and speedy help doesn't always come through with a quick solution.

The strangest of all who pray, are those who demand help. When not quickly answered some throw temper tantrums. Others threaten all manner of retaliatory actions such as; *becoming an atheist, smashing a plaster statue of their patron saint, declaring never again to pray, or to set foot in church.*

On the opposite extreme are those with strong religious convictions who don't get discouraged while waiting. Some even find the suspense exciting by trying to figure out the approach being used to answer their prayers.

An interesting example of prayer impatience appeared in the Jan-Feb '84 editon of Leaves (*for the address of the magazine, see App D*). The writer wanted to know:

"*...why some people's prayers are answered with very little effort, while others are left out completely...*"

The reply was both direct and amusing:

"*...Your question reminds me of the lady who went to a shrine seeking the gift of patience and her last five words were, 'and hurry up sending it..!'*"

Like so many of the other mysteries of religion, prayer is a mystery, and in many ways St. Jude is a mysterious figure. Nobody knows how the process of prayer works, or how St. Jude intercedes to help get petitions granted.

All we know is that everyday, countless people offer testimony to St. Jude's intercessory ability by placing paid *Thank You St. Jude* ads in world-wide publications.

A glance through metropolitan or *local newspapers, tabloids, shopping guides, the alternative underground press, and other publications* provides conclusive evidence that the "Patron Saint of Difficult and Hopeless Cases" gets results:

Whether famous or unknown, rich or poor, every so often we all need help with a desperate situation. But, there are individuals, even entire families who seem to go from one major calamity into another.

Some of these people react by becoming bitter, and hard. Others through prayer gain the gifts of insight, and wisdom.

The upcoming story is about Annette, a woman who has experienced a complex, difficult, and painful life until she discovered St. Jude in the newspaper. In a single statement, she summed up her feelings about all the heartache she has gone through:

"I now realize that God had to do something big to wake me up. I've been blessed, and no longer question whether a happening is a coincidence, or an answered prayer. I don't look for logical reasons for events, but faithfully accept what is."

Annette was a late arrival, born when her two brothers and sister were in their adolescent years. Her father was influential in her youth, and it's with him her story begins:

"My father was delighted with my birth. He was a Yankee from Vermont who had converted to the Catholic faith when he married my mother.

"He was very strong in his found religion. I recall how he warned many times that if I did anything wrong, *God would punish me.*"

Annette spoke about her mother as a hard worker who set a good example for her children. She explained:

"My mother was a first generation Polish-American, and quite knowledgeable about Catholicism.

"When I was a young girl, and talked to my parents, and other authoritative people about religion, what they said was frightening because they spoke of God as a strict disciplinarian. It seemed the only purpose for the practice of religion was to prepare for death.

"The message was clear, *be good and you go to heaven; goof up and you go to hell.* Like so many others, I practiced my religion out of fear.

"Every time I went to receive Holy Communion I was scared because I never felt deserving. I sincerely wanted to receive, yet I frantically repeated over and over; '*Make me worthy. Make me worthy.*'"

As a child Annette went to Church more often, and was much more sensitive to Jesus' suffering than friends her own age.
She recalled the time a nun, who had been teaching Catechism, told the story of the Crucifixion.

"I was the only one in my class who was moved to tears. The story really affected me. I remember going home, and praying to Jesus to allow me to do something to share His suffering."

Even with Annette's devout religious upbringing, in her adolescence she gradually lost her faith, and stopped attending Mass.

"I went off with the crowd and was having a grand old time. At eighteen I got a job as a typesetter. Before long I became the supervisor of typesetting. When the owners found out I was good with figures, they transferred me to the office. They later paid my way through accounting school.

"I put a lot of effort into that course, and enjoyed my work as well as my studies. I wasn't career minded and never thought of it as building a future. Accounting just interested me."

At the age of 21, Annette got married to a non-practicing Catholic.

"Even though my husband, Rick, went to parochial school, he was quite cynical, and questioned the motives of the Church. He'd say; '*All they ever ask for is money.*'

"I wanted children very badly. When I was 22, I gave birth to my first child, Audrey. She was the apple of my dad's eye. Sadly, he died three months after her birth. I was very affected by his death for I dearly loved and missed him very much.

"The next year Scott was born, followed by Leslie. I had three children in less than 26 months. I was determined everything would be perfect. But, things didn't work out that way."

Audrey was later diagnosed as having early infantile autism, a rare and severe mental disorder occurring in one child in 30,000.

Leslie became another problem. When she hadn't sat up by her first birthday, Annette suspected something was wrong. A routine examination concluded with a strong suspicion that Leslie had brain damage.

She was tentatively diagnosed as retarded with an emotional overlay. In simple terms, Annette's youngest child also had a mental illness.

Scott was the only one of the three children who appeared to have no abnormalities. Annette explained how she felt about her daughters:

"I was a devoted mother who suffered from a horrible guilt. My father's warnings, that if I did anything wrong *God would punish me,* kept going through my mind.

"Well, I had stopped going to church. So, out of fear, I returned to my religion, and began attending regular Sunday Masses.

"During the week I had to have something to occupy my time besides being a housewife and mother. I needed to get out, go to work and still be able to take care of my children.

"At that time I still wasn't seeking a career, just something that would interest me. I held a few office jobs working in the cost accounting departments of various manufacturing firms.

"When Audrey was four years old she went totally mute, and was incorrectly diagnosed as severely retarded.

"We searched around for any kind of treatment that might help her. Eventually, we found a psychiatrist who treated her very effectively with an amphetamine drug *dexedrine.* Today it's considered outmoded treatment. All I can say is I'm thankful it was in vogue when Audrey needed it.

"Life gets complicated, and my devotion to God didn't last. As before, I lapsed away from the Church because being inside gave me claustrophobia which made me very ill.

"In 1969, Audrey began speaking again. At the time I didn't have the *wisdom* to recognize that it was a gift from God. You see, a large percentage of autistic children who go mute, never speak again.

"When Audrey was six years old she seemed to be coming along nicely. Then the school authorities decided to place her in a special class for retarded children.

"I tried to make them understand that Audrey needed a special teacher, someone who was firm, patient and knowledgeable. They wouldn't listen to reason. I was absolutely disgusted and frustrated."

During the next two years the pressure of dealing with her daughters' handicaps overwhelmed her, and she was about to hit bottom. Slowly Annette explained the event that pushed her over the edge:

"My niece Julia, whom I loved like my own, had planned to be married. Six weeks before the wedding her fiance called it off. She still loved him, and later they ran off together. Julia didn't write or telephone, so naturally the family was worried.

"I knew where she was, so I wrote and gave her advice about coming home, or at least letting her parents know how she was doing.

"That did it. She telephoned her mother and said that she was indignant because '*mean old aunt Annette*' had scolded her. My brother's wife called me up screaming and demanding to know who I thought

I was sticking my nose in her daughter's personal affairs.

"I should've realized that my sister-in-law was only reacting out of worry. After all, the letter worked and Julia did call home. But, my reasoning was way off, and my self image was already at rock bottom. Julia was simply the crowning blow. Suddenly everything was too much to digest.

"I slipped to the very depths of despair. No matter what I did I couldn't climb out. I knew I wasn't right, and was sure I'd gone mad.

"By *September 1971*, I was so spaced out with a nervous breakdown that my doctor put me in the hospital. I was severely depressed, experiencing weird visions, and convinced I was going to die.

"I'll always remember the moment I handed myself over into God's care. I was lying on the hospital bed saying to myself, '*I just cannot do it alone.*' It was a complete letting go, and a trusting in God's will. From that point I started to come back. A powerful force took over, much greater than myself.

"I didn't hear any voices, yet, if I mentally posed a question, an answer would come to me. Sometimes the answers were veiled. When I was confused I'd mentally say, '*I don't understand.*' Immediately, a thought would come back; '*It's not to be revealed to you now.*'

"My main worry was for my children, and two of the answers concerned them. One was that Audrey would be OK; the other was He had a special place for Leslie.

"There's no question, God took over and I worked hand-in-hand with Him. I couldn't have made it by myself.

"While I was struggling to regain my sanity, I received a letter from my youngest brother's wife who is very religious. She meant well by writing; *'Everything happens for a reason.'* I remember saying; *'Thanks lady, I need this.'*

"In less than three months I was well enough to go home. When I explained to my doctors that I believed God carried me all the way, they tried to convince me that the medical explanation for what I was thinking was nothing more than a manifestation of my illness.

"As far as I'm concerned, they're entitled to their opinion and I'm entitled to mine.

"I now understand that what happened to me, happened for a reason. God accomplished a lot. He brought me back to my religion, and made one hell of a fighter out of me.

"For a long time I referred to my life as before, and after my breakdown. Even though I'd been very sick, I'm grateful for having gone through the experience because it changed my attitude, increased my *wisdom* and gave me greater *insight.*

"My doctor didn't want me staying at home all the time, so as part of my after care treatment he recommended I find a part time job. As he suggested I went to work in a local convenience store.

"It was simple and enjoyable, that is until the evening a man came in with a gun. He ordered me into the back room. I was scared to death because I was sure he was going to shoot me. I stayed in the back of the store a long time.

"That did it, I wasn't going to work there any longer. It wasn't worth it. I went out and found a job as a full charge bookkeeper.

"In the meantime, we were having problems with Leslie. Nobody in the school system seemed to know what to do with her. She was placed in special classes, then put in the first grade, and later even promoted to a fifth grade social studies class. Where they came up with that idea, I'll never understand. When that didn't work out, they bounced her around and around.

"I'll always remember one of the happiest moments after my breakdown. It was February '72 when I received a note that Audrey's teacher wanted to see me. When I arrived, she told me that something unusual had happened.

"It seemed that within the past few weeks Audrey had changed, and was doing fine. She explained that my daughter no longer belonged in her special class. She asked if I had any objections to having her transferred to a normal class.

"The first year the teachers sugar coated Audrey's marks by giving her '*A's*. The second year they didn't sugar coat them, and she still got '*A's*. She went to summer camp, and did just about everything I'd always hoped for. I hadn't forgotten how God revealed to me in the hospital that Audrey would be alright.

"For the three years, 1972 to 1975, my other daughter, Leslie, hadn't been getting the kind of help she needed. We took her for evaluation to the new medical center at *Tufts University* in Boston. When the results came in, it was recommended that the best place for my daughter would be a residential school.

"With a minimum of bureaucratic runaround the school department approved Leslie's admittance to the prestigious *Devereux Residental School* in Rutland, Massachusetts.

"Even though six years had gone by since my breakdown, I knew when Leslie was placed in the

Harvard of schools for her kind of handicap and condition, God had kept His promise."

For two years, 1976 to 1978, things leveled off for Annette and her family. She went into public accounting in September 1977, and earned her "certification in taxes." However, in the interim, Annette again stopped going to church. Then came the year 1978 and another period when everything seemed to go wrong.

"Just as we thought we'd gone through it all, Audrey, who was entering adolescence, started slipping. It was recommended she go back into therapy. But, the treatments didn't help, and by the spring of '79 she was hospitalized with a mental breakdown. Within a couple of weeks, without any significant signs of improvement she was released from the hospital, and sent home."

Then, along came a brand new problem. Annette's son, Scott, who was in his early teens, started getting into a lot of trouble in grade school. Annette admitted not being overly concerned about his behavior:

"We attributed the cause for his not doing well in class to his being an above average intelligent boy without enough of a challenge to occupy his mind.

"But, the next summer, Scott went off the deep end. In the beginning, every once in a while he'd come home drunk. We knew most teenagers go through a beer drinking phase, and that's why we failed to recognize how threatening this was.

"One day, without benefit of a driver's license, Scott took the family car, and wrecked it in an accident. Thus began my son's troubles with the courts. Matters continued downhill, and every so often Scott didn't come home all night.

"The awakening shock came when we discovered marijuana, and narcotic pills in my son's room. I couldn't believe he was doing drugs.

"We rushed off to the police station, and in so many words were told, '*they were not interested.*' Only after pleading with them to find out who was feeding that stuff to the kids, did they admit the problem was too great to overcome.

"In the spring of *'81*, while trying to deal with my son's problem, the special education department of our school system was breathing down our necks. They were threatening to cut off my daughters funding because Leslie had been at *Devereux* for four years.

"Every year we fought the campaign to get her an extension; somehow every year we won. How we did it will always remain a mystery because special education money had become very tight. Most children were lucky to get one, or two years; the fact Leslie had been given four was a blessing in itself.

"All this time, Audrey was getting progressively worse. She'd been transferred from her normal class, back to a special class, and then into a class for retarded children.

"*Early in 1981*, my inner drive to succeed prompted me to accept a position as comptroller of a multi-million dollar corporation.

"It was a fast paced, high pressure job which demanded a lot of travel. The salary was excellent, I had my own company credit cards, and an expensively furnished office with a beautiful view of the Connecticut River.

"As long as my responsibilities were taken care of, I was allowed to come and go pretty much as I pleased. Everything was going fine until the impossible month of *October '81*.

"*On the first day*, Audrey was put in a short term care center suffering from schizophrenia.

"*The sixth day*, at four o'clock in the afternoon, my boss informed me that the corporation had been sold. He explained that the new management already had a comptroller, and couldn't use another. Regretfully, he said I was relieved, and then instructed me to clean out my desk before leaving at 4:30.

"Looking back, I should've been prepared. It was no secret that negotiations had been going on to sell the corporation, but I refused to think about it.

"*Back in '81* it wasn't easy for a woman to get a comptrollers position. Besides we had gotten used to having the incomes of two to meet our living expenses.

"Out of desperation, I decided to open my own accounting business. I still don't know what possessed me to do such a thing considering how little self-confidence I had. It had never even been a dream of mine to have my own business. In fact, all I ever wanted was just a good, steady job.

"With the only piece of equipment I owned, a calculator, I went into business out of the basement of my home. It's rough starting from nothing and the money was slow in coming.

"*At the end of October '81*, Audrey was released from the hospital. The doctors told me that other than putting her back on her feet, there was little else they could do. They explained that my daughter needed long term care. The problem was, there were very few such centers.

"It was not abnormal for patients to wait as long as two years before an opening could be found at a hospital with a long term program. With the exception of sub-standard facilities, waiting lists were lengthy. We searched everywhere, and asked everybody to help.

"*On New Year's Day 1982,* I was desperate. That's when I noticed a Thank You St. Jude novena ad in the newspaper. It read; '*This novena has never been known to fail.*'

"For anyone in my situation those words had a strong attraction. Terrific, that was exactly what I needed, *satisfaction guaranteed.* I cut out the novena prayer to St. Jude, and began reciting it.

"During the next few days, I made a lot of novenas to the 'Patron Saint of Desperate and Hopeless Cases.' With each prayer I pleaded with St. Jude to help me find a long term care facility for Audrey.

"I remember calling my mother and weeping from the depths of my heart. Even at nearly 80 years of age she was praying to a long list of saints. She was always praying for me, or writing to one religious group or another to have Masses said in my behalf.

"Three months went by, and then the mental health department called to tell me *The Four Winds Hospital* in New York State had an opening for Audrey. It was a long shot because the possibility of getting the special education director in my town to approve out of state hospital funding was just about zero.

"We'd checked everywhere else, so why not check this one out. We had nothing to lose, besides it sounded like a nice place to visit.

"A couple of days later we took Audrey to New York to meet with the therapist. Immediately, I knew it was right, and without asking anyone for permission I had her admitted.

"The following day I spoke to the special education director. He had a lot of power because it was his department which approved, or disapproved out of state educational funding.

"After explaining what I had done, he became upset and told me I should have waited because *The Four Winds Hospital* was not on the Massachusetts' pre-approved list.

"Well, to make a complicated story short, even though the possibility of getting the necessary funding was extremely remote, the hospital was approved. Moreover, Audrey was provided with a private tutor.

"That was my first experience with St. Jude, but, it left no doubt in my mind that he works *very powerfully*.

"Leslie and Audrey were set, at least for the time being; Scott was another problem. For almost a year my son went through a series of arrests, for minor incidents, usually fighting or disturbing the peace.

"One night when he left the house he was so high on drugs he had no idea of what he was doing. I was sure something terrible would happen to him. I threw myself down on my knees, and begged St. Jude to protect him. The next thing we heard, Scott had been picked up by the police while strolling down the middle of a busy road.

"I remember the way I found out my son had a serious drinking problem. The lawyer who was handling one of Scott's many court appearances, told us that my boy's behavior pattern was that of an alcoholic.

"I was stunned because I'd always thought of alcoholics as derelicts who slept in vacant buildings and rummaged through trash cans.

"Yet, the enormity of my son's problem didn't hit me until after I had taken him for treatment to several facilities. I'd never dreamed such conditions existed. In every waiting room were nine and ten year old alcoholics, and drug addicts.

"That July ('82) we put Scott in a hospital for alcoholics in New Hampshire. We could have saved the trouble because the three weeks he spent there were not very productive.

"Every time he went out of the house, I did not know if he'd come back alive. His reactions were so violent. Whenever he stayed away from home for several days, and returned safe I'd place a *Thank You St. Jude* ad in the newspaper.

"At times I was too embarrassed to pray for help. There were so many problems over which I had no control or solutions. I felt like all I was doing was asking St. Jude to give me this, and give me that.

"One day Scott volunteered to join the local *Alcoholics Anonymous* group. As long as he attended the regular meetings he was fine. But, every so often he'd lull himself into thinking that one drink wouldn't hurt and off he'd go.

"In the meantime, once again we'd run out of extensions with the school department for Leslie. The officials at *Devereux* wrote that it was vital my daughter be given one more year. After that she'd be ready to leave.

"The answer was, '*no more time.*' Leslie's funding was cut off. Our only recourse was a hearing scheduled for *December '82.*

"That fall I decided to go to *Spafford Hall,* a hospital in New Hampshire where they taught families to cope with relative's alcoholism. At the time it seemed like a good idea because I realized I needed the rest.

"But, when I returned home I discovered Scott had wrecked another family car. I was sick, and in the throes of my second breakdown. I had been working long hours trying to get my business off the ground.

"There was the pressure of Leslie's upcoming hearing; Audrey had suffered a severe relapse in the hospital; and Scott was acting like a jerk, doing drugs and alcohol, and being hauled into court every time we turned around.

"In October (*'82*), I suffered another breakdown. Thankfully it was mild, and my doctor arranged to have me cared for at home by rotating shifts of mental health workers.

"This one lasted only a few weeks, but it was then things started to be revealed to me again. A feeling came over me. I knew there would be a healing in my family, and my existing problems were going to be resolved.

"I had an exaggerated sense that I loved everybody. One morning I woke up Scott, and repeated over and over again that I loved him. He pleaded with me to stop. That day, he went out and found a job.

"Every morning he got up at *5:30,* made his lunch, and walked to and from work. It was a long distance, about 10 miles round trip.

"When Leslie's hearing came up in *December,* our lawyer met with the school board's attorney, and somehow convinced them to grant my daughter one more year at *Devereux.*

"St. Jude came through again. I was grateful to God, and the number of novenas to my powerful patron saint steadily increased.

"Since my doctor understood how much I enjoyed my work, he decided the best medicine would be to get me back to my business.

"It was still a growing enterprise with a painfully slow cash flow. I realized that worrying about money was the last thing I needed. I reasoned that the best solution would be to get a dependable job with a steady paycheck and either close my business after the *'83 tax season* or run it as an investment.

"For guidance I made another novena to St. Jude, and asked for his help. Within days I located a perfect job, about *32* hours a week; exactly what I needed.

"During the day I worked part time, and at night I ran my business. Three months later that little job turned out to be of vital importance because my husband had been laid-off, and went on unemployment compensation.

"Once again I was regularly attending Mass, but my old problem about receiving the Eucharist continued. Unexpectedly, one Sunday morning, as I got up from the pew to go to Communion, something comforting washed over me. In an instant, I understood God didn't want me to be afraid. All the fear and trepidation I'd known for most of my life vanished.

"*In the early summer of '83,* Scott, and one of his friends got into a fight with a young man who had hitched a ride with them. They were arrested on charges of assault with a dangerous weapon (*kicking*); unarmed robbery (*the young man said he was missing five-dollars*); and a threat of murder, (*in the heat of the fight Scott said he'd kill the young man.)*

"This time my son was in serious trouble because he was already on probation for fighting. The law was clear, seven to ten years in prison was the mandatory sentence for anyone violating probation with a serious charge.

"At the hearing our lawyer explained that because of Scott's prior conviction, the judge had no alternative but to send my son to prison. The trial was set for January '84.

"In the interim *(Oct '83)*, my husband's unemployment money ran out. We went from a difficult financial situation to one of sheer desperation. I found myself thrust into the position of chief family breadwinner.

"The New Year came quickly, and on the day of Scott's trial I prayed fervently to St. Jude not to let him go to prison.

"Are you ready for this. In the courtroom, our lawyer whispered that some official of the court, months earlier, had mistakenly taken my son off probation.

"Since there was no record, Scott got another chance. Instead of jail, the judge put him on three years probation. "St. Jude did indeed answer my prayers; this time with a *miracle*."

EPILOGUE

"Leslie has come home from *Devereux,* is enrolled in a special class in a local school system, and she is doing very well.

"Audrey was released from *The Four Winds Hospital* in May '84 with an encouraging prognosis. She's in her twenties, survived a serious mental illness, lives in her own apartment, and has earned her high school diploma. She has a lot of determination, and is fighting hard to pull herself back to normalcy. With St. Jude's support I know she'll make it.

"With the help of an advisor-friend, my business has rapidly grown the way I'd dreamed it would. I'll soon be leaving my part time job to devote full time to my business.

"At this writing the healing process for my family, disclosed to me during my breakdowns is happening. My religious faith has been restored; I fully trust in God. My fear of the Almighty has dissolved. In its place has come a knowledge of His mercy.

"St. Jude has blessed me over and over again; too many times to publish a *Thank You* prayer in the newspapers for each request granted. So, I offer this, my life story, as a special gift to my powerful patron.

"Thank You St. Jude, I've had so many of my requests granted. *Publication Promised.*"

CHAPTER III

CITY OF HOPE AND FAITH

Loyalty, dedication, and an everlasting bond of friendship are a few of the characteristics which set St. Jude's friends apart from devotees of other saints.

For some undefined reason, once prayers have been answered through St. Jude, most people get an overpowering impulse to publicly express appreciation.

When it comes to showing gratitude to the "Patron Saint of the Desperate" apparently personal preference dictates the rule.

Annette took her obligation to thank St. Jude a step beyond the average by baring her soul on paper. Others choose to put their feelings of thankfulness into letter form.

Every week hundreds of pounds of *thank you* mail is received at St. Jude Shrines and Mass Leagues throughout the civilized world.

The outpouring of gratefulness involves such personal matters as:

A happy marriage, success in business or employment, health, a return of faith, reconciliation with a marriage partner, a cure of alcoholism or drug addiction, peace of mind, a safe pregnancy or an uncomplicated birth, the return of an absent family member, a peaceful death, and a multitude of other granted favors.

Some St. Jude devotees believe that appreciation can only be properly expressed by the performance of a *good deed, or a work of mercy.*

These people go out of their way to run errands for shut-ins, or the aged; volunteer to help the sick, or less fortunate; take part in charitable events like the annual Danny Thomas, St. Jude Hospital Fund Raising Drive.

A number of devotees believe gratitude must be expressed in *material ways.* Perhaps this is why so many statues of the patron saint have been donated to churches, or for the extraordinary growth of front yard shrines.

Yet, of all the ways devotees elect to say thank you to St. Jude, the rarest is *total dedication of self.*

This elite group, not only gives generously of time, energy, and money, but expresses their appreciation in monumental ways.

Danny Thomas is certainly such a person; another was the Reverend Harold Purcell, (*affectionately known as Father Harold*).

The following inspirational story is about this remarkable priest who was born on January 3, 1881 and christened Thomas Joseph. He was the fourth boy of eleven children; the last born to Nicholas and Mary Purcell.

When he was a lad of four, (*1885*), his father was killed in a coal mining accident. In 1894 the Purcells moved from Girardville, Pennsylvania to Philadelphia.

At the age of sixteen, March 14, 1897, Tom was accepted into the Passionist Congregation, and given a new name, *Confrater Harold* for (*Harold of the Sorrowful Virgin*).

For seven years the novice was involved in intense study for the priesthood. On December 17,

1904, *Confrater Harold* was ordained, *Father Harold Purcell, C.P.*

From the onset, the young Passionist gained a reputation for aggressiveness and stubborn determination.

He was gifted with a positive, pleasing, and persuasive personality which he used skillfully to win support for his causes. The energetic priest wasn't shy when it came to speaking his mind.

On the surface Father Harold was gruff, but in truth was a gentle man who had a tender compassion for the poor, and downtrodden.

With absolute confidence he accepted all difficult challenges, never allowing even major obstacles to defeat him. In September 1912, while on assignment in Illinois, the missionary fell victim to diabetes mellitus.

> *Diabetes was ranked the third major killer until 1922, when control of the chronic disease was made possible through the discovery of insulin.*

Proper rest and careful attention to a rigid diet was prescribed. But, Father Harold was a traveling missionary who considered such advice an impractical nuisance. For the next nine years he ate on the run; from every kind of menu.

In March 1921, Father Harold's superior ask him to take on a project of starting a national magazine designed to generate support for the Passionist's China missions.

Even though the 40 year old priest wanted the assignment, when told the magazine was to be strictly a devotional publication, he promptly rejected the offer.

In his typical direct manner, he explained that to be successful, the publication would have to deal with current events of interest to Catholics.

It should serve as a commentary on social and economic issues, answer theological questions while providing family entertainment through good literature.

His superior wasn't in favor of the approach, but after failing every argument he reluctantly conceded defeat and gave his blessings to the project.

Five months later *(Aug 1921)* the first issue of *the* Sign *(for the sign of the Cross)* went out to *300* paid subscribers.

As the editor, it was Father Harold's responsibility to get every edition of the magazine out on schedule.

Deadline after deadline saw the ill priest writing well into the early morning hours. No matter how long he worked, if he failed to appear at the six o'clock breakfast community prayer, his superior sent for him.

Without a word of complaint, the weary Passionist obediently joined his brothers.

By 1924 *the Sign* was a tremendous success with a paid circulation of 70,000 subscribers. Larger facilities were needed to accommodate the growing magazine staff, so in the spring of 1925, Father Harold set out on a fund raising campaign.

He wheeled, dealed, and begged until he collected enough money to erect a two story yellow brick building.

It was Father Harold's firm belief that *God helps those who help themselves.* In the May 1926 edition of *the Sign,* in a few lines he spelled out his personal philosophy:

Seventeen year old Confrater Harold of the Sorrowful Virgin, C.P., - Mar. 1898.

Passionist Missionary, Father Purcell - 1915.

A New Venture

WITH THIS ISSUE OF SIGN, the Passionist Fathers present to American Catholics a new monthly magazine. It is their ambition to publish a periodical which, both in physical makeup and intellectual content, will be worthy of the interested approval of its actual and prospective readers. SIGN, in common with other Catholic publications, purposes to disseminate truth, to combat the thousand and one errors confronting Catholics at every turn, to interpret, from a Catholic viewpoint, significant current events, and to offset, in some measure, the pernicious influences of the lurid secular press.

To this end, it publishes instructive expositions of the doctrines of holy Church, pertinent articles on present-day issues, live discussions of industrial, social, and economic questions, and refreshing and wholesome literary entertainment.

We feel that this new venture must have the cordial approval of the American hierarchy, who, in setting aside last March as Catholic Press Month, convincingly stressed the need of a strong Catholic press and cogently appealed to the Catholic conscience to support such a press. Unfortunately, this appeal was more than necessary, for, as a matter of strict fact, less than 25 percent of Catholics in the United States read any Catholic periodical. Hence, any publication attempting to reach the remaining 75 percent of present nonreaders is a praiseworthy enterprise.

The distinguishing feature of SIGN is the prominence it gives the cross. Never was the setting forth of Christ Crucified so essential as in our own day, when the opportunities and means of pleasure so abound, when, to the non-Catholic, the cross is no longer a symbol but an empty decoration, when even our Catholic people are all too prone to substitute an easy-going piety for the stern gospel of self-denial. Wherefore, SIGN aims at holding up before the public none other than "the sign of the Son of Man"—the norm of Catholic thought and conduct.

Bearing in mind that there are over three thousand monthly publications in the United States, each loudly declaring its message, surely no apology is required for one that shall voice, however faintly, the appeal of our Saviour Crucified.

Father Harold Purcell, C.P.

"When a man enters into a partnership with the Almighty God, he should lay out a huge program. To be satisfied with a small project is to distrust either the personal interest or the active cooperation of his Divine Partner."

By *1932, Sign* had doubled to 64 pages, and was being mailed to a *105,000* paid subscribers.

Father Harold had great faith in the intercessory power of St. Jude. Occasionally during the 1920's and 1930's he'd offer *Sign* readers free printed St. Jude prayer cards.

He also published *Thank You St. Jude* letters from devotees who wanted to share the experience of their granted petitions.

As part of his daily spiritual prayers, Father Harold always asked his patron saint for the special protection of his Passionist brothers working in far away China.

For a number of years Father Harold had been obsessed with a dream to build an entire city in honor of St. Jude.

From a pencilled sketch, he had a painting made which was prominently displayed on his office wall.

Whenever visitors asked about the picture, they were treated to a lengthy description of a community with a church, school, clinic, hospital and settlement for the poor of the southeastern United States.

In the spring of 1934, Father Harold was introduced to Bishop Thomas J. Toolen of the Diocese of Mobile, Alabama. True to form, he told the bishop all about his dream settlement. Impressed by the priest's enthusiasm, Bishop Toolen extended an open invitation to Father Harold:

"If you ever need a bishop as a sponsor, you're welcome to come to Alabama."

That was all the encouragement the Passionist needed. Within twenty-four hours *(Mar 12, 1934)* he submitted a ten page letter to his superior requesting permission to go to Alabama to begin his project.

After waiting patiently for several days, Father Harold was disappointed when his petition was unconditionally denied.

In response, the determined priest formally applied for permission to leave the Passionist Order *(demissorial)* to seek acceptance as a diocesan priest.

With no alternative, on July 28th, Father Harold's superior approved the request.

For the first time in thirty years, the hard driving missionary was without the support of a religious community.

Except for a small cash settlement, customarily awarded to priests leaving the order, he was also without funds.

Father Harold's final act as editor of *Sign* was the composition of a combination farewell-appeals letter for publication in the upcoming issue of the magazine:

"My Dear Friends: After many years of thought and prayer about the matter, I enter upon the realization of a long cherished ambition to work personally and directly among the poor Negroes of the south...

"...May I ask you, my friends, to help me to help them (poor, undernourished and neglected colored children of Alabama)? I shall be more than grateful for even the least offering you send me.

> *"And Our Lord Himself will reward a hundredfold your charity to these least of His brethren. You can count on that.*
> *"Please forward your offering to me c/o The Sign, Union City, N.J."*

As the ailing priest's train pulled into the *Mobile, Alabama station* he knew full well it was not going to be easy.

Catholics represented only about *two percent* of all Alabamians. Like many of the white people, the black population feared and mistrusted priests and nuns.

Also, the secret terrorist organization, the *Ku Klux Klan,* targeted those it considered to be alien-outsiders, such as: *Negroes, Jews, and in particular Catholics.*

As for money to finance his venture, Father Harold was on his own. When Bishop Toolen accepted him into his fold he left no room for question:

> *"You are most welcome in the Diocese of Mobile. However, you must understand our conditions. We cannot help you financially or take responsibility for debts you may incur, nevertheless I am at your service in any other way."*

As a consequence of his diabetes, the gray, balding priest had developed severe circulation problems.

Leg pains forced him to rely heavily on a cane to walk. It was a struggle just getting down the two steps to the station platform.

After only a few days of rest, Father Harold was out on a walking tour through Montgomery's slums.

Upon seeing the unsanitary living conditions of the poor, he became more determined than ever to find a site where he could build his *City of Hope and Faith* in honor of St. Jude.

By the end of August 1934, he'd found what seemed to be a perfect location. The property was a large field on the eastern edge of Montgomery known as the *Hunter Vaughn Estate.*

Meanwhile, the response to his farewell letter, published in the August edition of *Sign,* produced encouraging results in the form of greatly needed financial donations.

"With renewed vigor, Father Harold returned to New York to launch a fund raising campaign. He took on an exhausting schedule, traveling the northeast and midwest describing the inhumane conditions the poor were living under in the Montgomery area.

Time and again he repeated what he'd seen in a slum district known as *Shuffle Alley.* Audiences gasped in shock when he told how one outhouse, and a single cold water pump served the needs of more than a hundred men, women, and children.

Vividly, the gifted priest described seeing the twenty, one-room shacks, each housing as many as seven people.

He recounted being appalled when he looked inside the shacks. In one was an old black man nearing death; lying on a pile of rags on a dirt floor. In another hut, a seriously ill young girl, undernourished, and crippled with tuberculosis.

He explained that the sick were not being cared for because of a critical shortage of hospital beds, as well as trained personnel.

To meet the medical needs of the entire black Montgomery community were five doctors, two dentists, four nurses, and five midwives.

Contributing to the problem were the *Jim Crow Laws* which directed the segregation of races in public places, facilities, and hospitals.

The rulings restricted the treatment of the black population to one hospital and an infirmary. More than 500 black adults were in desperate need of immediate major surgery.

During the final quarter of 1934, the ailing priest had spoken to so many groups about his plans for the *City of St. Jude* he was often hoarse.

Long periods of standing in front of audiences caused his varicose veins to swell to the bursting point. The pain was unbearable.

He ignored colds which lingered on for many months. Friends worried about his deteriorating health, and tried to convince him to rest.

The driven priest knew they were right, but continued involving himself with things needing his personal attention.

Sunday mornings he went from one Catholic service to another. With permission of the pastors, he spoke to as many congregations as possible. Every group was begged for donations; when necessary he even took up the collections himself.

Between exhausting speaking engagements, Father Harold spent hours on the telephone with clerical, and lay friends talking about *the city of hope and faith*.

When not on the phone he was sending out letters:

"One cent will buy a dose of medicine. One nickel will buy two diapers. We need shirts, stomach bands, nightgowns.

"Another nickel will buy twelve cotton swabs or one pint of milk.

"Eight cents, a loaf of bread, a can of corn or tomatos, some rice, cornmeal, spaghetti, beans or potatoes.

"Ten cents will get a child a square meal, properly balanced to correct malnutrition.

"Send us clothing, new or old; bolts or remnants, we can use anything."

His pleas produced remarkable results. Within a few weeks bundles and bales of clothing; boxes of canned and packaged goods; even letters stuffed with donations arrived daily at *the Sign* building in New Jersey.

With supplies and funds coming in, Father Harold set his sights on convincing a couple of experienced nurses to give a year to a proposed St. Jude dispensary.

Whenever he interviewed a candidate, he concluded with these few words of caution:

"It will be a hard year. You won't have any social life; you'll be working day and night; very little pay, just room and board; and limited time for relaxation."

Back in Montgomery, word spread about the plan to purchase the *Hunter Vaughn Estate,* and convert it into a medical facility for the poor.

Strong opposition arose. Batches of telegrams were sent to St. Jude's priest warning him not to carry out his plans. Angry neighbors let it be known it would be dangerous for all concerned if he refused to listen to reason.

It was a difficult decision because Father Harold was a tough priest who never ran away from a good fight. But, he had to consider the safety of the black community, so he decided to terminate negotiations for the property.

A few weeks later he heard about the possibility of renting part of a late 19th century, three story house in a quiet, white middle class neighborhood at 1015 *Hull Street* between Cramer and Highland Court.

It wasn't exactly an ideal location for St. Jude's clinic because it was too far from the people he wanted to serve.

From his New York City headquarters, Father Harold carried out negotiations by telephone, and mail. Soon the rental terms were agreed to, and the deal was made.

Donated packages and other goods which were piled in *the Sign* building were shipped to *Hull Street*.

By December 11, 1934, volunteers were busily sorting bundles and bales of clothing, boxes of canned and packaged goods, housewares, vestments, and other supplies.

But, *Hull Street* was not to be. Within the week the house was burglarized with everything of value stolen.

News of the break-in alerted the neighbors about the proposed clinic to treat the poor. A protest committee was quickly organized. The burglary, neighborhood opposition, and location convinced Father Harold to once again set out in search for a more suitable, temporary building for St. Jude's dispensary.

Early in 1935, the determined priest found a 40 acre wooded lot for sale. It was a beautiful property, known as the *Dimmick Estate.*

It had been a thriving plantation and was perfect for the *City of St. Jude,* smack in the middle of the black community on *Fairview Avenue,* in the western section of Montgomery, known as *Washington Terrace.*

An agreement to purchase was drawn up with the first installment of *$8,440* due by July, l5th, or the deal would be called off.

Meanwhile, Father Harold continued his search for a large building that would serve as a temporary St. Jude dispensary.

Finding a suitable location seemed an impossible task, so he turned to the "Patron Saint of Desperate and Hopeless Cases" for help.

Before the end of May *(1935),* Father Harold's prayers were answered, as he was lead to a large ten room house in a densely populated all black neighborhood.

The most important feature of the property was nobody cared what went on at the 614 *Holt Street* dwelling because it was a *house of prostitution.*

Before the Great Depression the house had been one of more than *275* thriving Montgomery houses of prostitution which catered almost exclusively to white males.

However, massive unemployment resulted in a scarcity of spare money. The ladies who had worked in the house were forced to leave for richer territories. A few even went into legitimate occupations.

The madame-owner of the house was a white woman who occupied and operated the pleasure establishment.

In a pouring rain, Father Harold took a taxi to the *Holt Street* address determined to rent the property.

No matter how many times he repeated the story, his eyes twinkled with devilment. He always began with the madame's name, "*Annie Jerusalem O'Toole*" (*not her real name*) and her reaction when she opened the door:

> "*You all go 'way. This place, if ya all don't know it, has a terrible reputation. It gives me the creeps to see ya standing here. I never had no religion and I don't want any now.*"

Father Harold just smiled warmly, and before Annie knew what had happened, he'd talked his way inside.

Looking around as if he'd already taken possession, the sly old priest casually mentioned he needed the house for *St. Jude's* mission.

Annie began to tremble. Taking him by the arm she led him to a bedroom where a small white boy was sleeping.

She explained that one of her girls had been the boy's mother. As the woman was dying she told Annie *a saint would come for her son.*

Annie admitted to being scared half to death when he mentioned that saint's name. In his typical take charge manner, Father Harold told Annie he'd be back the next morning to baptize the boy. He said he knew of a family who'd be delighted to adopt the lad, with no questions asked.

Before leaving, the persuasive priest convinced Annie to lease the house for $50.00 a month. As part of the deal he agreed to help her begin a new respectable life by finding her a decent job in another city.

During the early weeks of May 1935, volunteers from a Montgomery Catholic church cleaned the Holt Street house. Everything that hadn't been taken was moved from *Hull Street.*

The spacious living room in the rear of the dwelling was converted into a chapel to comfortably serve 50 people.

To let everyone know the house had changed its mission, a hand-painted muslin banner was staked across the front lawn reading; THIS IS THE CITY OF ST. JUDE.

A couple of weeks later, two recruited nurses arrived from New York City. Also three doctors from Montgomery *(Dr. John Martin, a protestant; Dr. Clarence Weil, a Jew; and Dr. R. T. Adair, a black physician)* volunteered their services to the clinic.

With everything ready, on a rainy *Sunday, June 2, 1935, St. Jude's Catholic Dispensary* was officially dedicated.

At the open house ceremony, Father Harold told a small gathering that this was only the beginning of the City of St. Jude.

The amazing priest now had to divide his efforts between fund raising in the northeast, and directing the dispensary in the southeast.

Every month he had to come up with $500 to meet the basic operating expenses of the mission, as well as raise $8,440 for the first installment payment on the *Fairview Avenue forty acre property.*

That fall *(Oct 1935),* the first volunteer priest, *Father Hubert Joseph Roberge* arrived to help Father Harold run the clinic.

As the year drew to an end, it was obvious St. Jude's Catholic Dispensary was a success. Within its first six months of operation, more than 800 ragged, hungry, sick, needy poor people had been treated.

On opening day, volunteer Nurses - Mary Brelsford and Marie Meredith in front of the clinic - June 2, 1935.

At Christmas time the two priests held a party for the children of the catechism classes. On Christmas Eve, Father Harold offered Midnight Mass in St. Jude's chapel for 35 people.

After the holiday season, Father Harold was again on a train northward bound. For months he ran a hectic fund raising schedule, traveling throughout the cold, windy midwest, and the damp northeast.

Never allowing a moment for relaxation, the St. Jude's priest grabbed meals on the run. His diabetes condition developed into a serious leg infection.

Stubborn determination wasn't enough, and on *April 17, 1936* he collapsed. Doctors at St. Mary's Hospital in Hoboken, New Jersey told him he had to have an immediate leg operation.

He refused saying too many things needed his immediate attention. Recuperation from surgery would be a waste of valuable time.

For nearly a month he was kept in the hospital; constantly complaining. All the while he continued conducting business from his bed.

Although still very ill, he checked himself out of St. Mary's; only to be brought back by ambulance two weeks later. This trip he underwent the leg surgery.

In his absence, Father Roberge was in charge of the dispensary. The young priest was having problems with two of the women volunteers, so he wrote to Father Harold for advice.

The reply didn't help much, but it surely must have brought a smile to the frustrated priest:

"Female psychology is the mystery. No man can possibly understand women. I'd been told that all my life; now I know it."

Just as soon as Father Harold was able to get out of his bed, he was out of the hospital, and back out on the fund raising trail.

As before, he never let-up. On July 15, 1936, Father Harold proudly made the down payment of $8,440 on the Fairview Avenue forty acre property.

On August 19, 1936, he made the final payment and received the deed for:

"...the southeastern quarter of the northeastern quarter of Section 23 of Township 16 and Range 17..."

A *Certificate of Incorporation*, filed on October 20, 1937, officially established the *City of St. Jude* as a non-profit business:

> *"...to promote education, religion, and to render benevolent aid to the needy, sick, injured or diseased, and to do other acts of charity for the needy..."*

With renewed energy, the priest's fund raising efforts picked up momentum. Now he was out to gather a sizable building fund.

In 1937, Father Richard J. Cushing *(later Archbishop of Boston; made Cardinal by Pope John XXIII in 1958)* became a close friend of Father Harold; later becoming a major supporter of the *City of St. Jude*.

When time came for construction of St. Jude's church, with loving care he selected a slight rise in the center of the site.

Until additional buildings could be erected, the church basement was to serve as an elementary school, as well as the sister's living quarters.

For months Father Harold had been on a recruiting campaign for sisters to staff the St. Jude Parochial School.

He didn't want nuns who'd be content sitting inside the institution shut away from society in clausura *(cloister)*.

Besides organizing social activities for the youth, St. Jude's nuns would have to become a living part of the community; going out to the people in their homes.

In August 1938 with the church-school-convent nearing completion, a dozen *Sisters of the Holy Family of Nazareth* arrived. They had been reassigned from Chicago's Polish neighborhoods to form the heart of the teaching staff.

But, before they could settle into their unfinished quarters, Father Harold called on them to take charge of student registration. It was an enormous project requiring the interviewing of hundreds of parents or guardians.

By the time the sisters had finished, 275 black children were enrolled in the first four grades of the *St. Jude Parochial School.*

Since most of the parents couldn't afford school uniforms, the sisters, with the help of several mothers and grandmothers, labored day and night so each child could be wearing the school colors on opening day.

Excitement mounted as the first day of school neared. It had taken Father Harold four-and-one half years to raise enough money to operate a dispensary, purchase land, and construct St. Jude's church-school.

It was an impressive structure, architecturally designed after the fourth century *Sancta Maria church in Cosmedin in Rome.*

On the front of the tall bell tower, stretching up 105 feet, was a sculptured, white marble scene of the Crucifixion.

In tribute to St. Mary, a blue tiled roof was put on the church, which from a distance looked like a window in the sky.

Everywhere throughout the interior were signs of the great love Father Harold had for St. Jude.

The Ten Commandments were carefully engraved on heavy wooden ceiling crossbeams. Portrayed

Beautiful St. Jude Church as it looks today.

along the walls were hand carved statues of Jesus' Mother, St. Jude, St. Benedict the Moor, St. Joseph, St. Monica, the Sacred Heart of Jesus, St. Augustine, St. Martin, and Blessed Charles Lwanga *(canonized in 1964)*.

When asked about the Negro statue of the Beatified Lwanga, Father Harold enjoyed telling how the holy man, and twenty-one other black African Christians, had been martyred in Uganda between 1885 and 1887.

Father Harold's favorite object was a large hand engraving of the Last Supper which covered the entire face of the Appalachian oak altar Communion table. Encased within the altar were relics of St. Peter, and the Blessed Lwanga.

On October 27, 1938, hundreds of well-wishers were present when Bishop Toolen dedicated the completed *St. Jude Church and Parochial School.*

Father Harold involved himself in every phase of the school. He posted a long list of rules of behavior, and manners which every student was required to memorize.

He regularly visited the classrooms and approved of the strict, yet loving approach to discipline. Every child was taught self-respect by the message:

> *"Don't ever hate the white folk. If they treat you wrong, you act right, anyway. Sooner or later together we are going to change the way things are; not by hate, but by love."*

The wise priest wanted to help poor families, yet everybody knew he was opposed to giving people *something for nothing.*

Every parent was required to pay *30 cents* a week, plus *15 cents* a day for the milk and hot lunch program for each child enrolled in St. Jude's.

Children of the parents who couldn't afford the tuition or food, were assigned after school jobs of cleaning the church, mowing the lawn, and other tasks around the grounds. Some students worked after school, or weekends stuffing appeal envelopes for 15 cents and hour.

> *No child was denied an education; no child ever went hungry; and no child was given a free ride.*

The *Sisters of the Holy Family of Nazareth* became Father Harold's community as he assumed full responsibility for their food, shelter, money and other needs.

When not away on fund raising tours, he celebrated early morning Mass with his nuns, and at every opportunity had lunch with them. They thought of their pastor as a unique leader, superior, director, and beloved friend.

Early in 1939, the second building of the *City of St. Jude,* a two-story social center, was erected directly behind the church.

St. Jude Social Center - 1939, a multi-purpose building

St. Jude's Catholic Dispensary on Holt Street was permanently closed after everything had been moved to the new social center.

In the spring of 1939, Father Harold heard about nearby Autauga County with a population of *70,000* people, but not a single Roman Catholic among them. As far as he was concerned that was mission country.

Wasting no time, he purchased some property in Marbury, a town about 25 miles northwest the *City of St. Jude.*

Immediately, he began negotiations with the *Vincentian Sisters of Charity* of Perrysville, Pennsylvania to assign nuns to teach the children and adults, care for the sick, and operate a proposed dispensary in Marbury.

Meanwhile, St. Jude's school had become too crowded. Father Harold was concerned that in the future some children might have to be refused admission.

In his most ambitious endeavor to date, the tired old priest went to his roster of good Samaritans which had grown to more than *80,000.* With determination he sent letters, and telephoned as many benefactors as possible.

He explained the space problem at the school, and asked each to dig deep into their pockets for generous donations because $400,000 was needed. *(Equivalent to nearly three-and-a-half-million dollars in mid-1980's money).*

Nobody believed Father Harold had a chance of collecting such an incredible sum. After all, the nation was still struggling to climb out of the depths of the Depression.

Through perseverance, in *1940* construction got underway on a *600* student, *32* class, *St. Jude Educational Institute.*

In June, seven Vincentian nuns were assigned to the Marbury mission where they saw poverty, *"the likes of which defied description."*

The first obstacle they had to face was prejudice. Many Marbury citizens feared Catholics, especially the women draped in black.

With faith, courage, and kindness the sisters overcame much of the hostility, and in time won the confidence of most of the people.

The Marbury project, called *The Holy Ghost Catholic Mission Center,* began with a tiny chapel which served double duty as a school.

A *Home for Incurables* for those with no source of income or assistance was added. Small rooms, clean beds, and care with dignity was provided for the crippled, paralyzed, feeble, aged, and dying.

Father Harold sent his top construction crew to the daughter mission of the *City of St. Jude* to erect a brick nursing home.

At the same time, building was moving at full speed on the 330 foot long, two-story *St. Jude Educational Institute.*

Suddenly the United States was involved in a World War. Civilian construction came to an abrupt standstill as building materials, and manpower were sent off to war.

Even with building interrupted, St. Jude's priest was busier than ever. In *1943*, he bought a vacant school on Montgomery's north side for a *Nazareth Catholic Mission.*

More about this daughter mission of the "City of St. Jude" in the upcoming chapter.

In the early months of 1943 Father Harold received one of his most fulfilling rewards. It happened on the day *Annie Jerusalem O'Toole* unexpectedly turned up at the city.

After the usual greetings between friends who hadn't seen each other in a long time, *Annie* rambled on about her old house on Holt Street, the weather, and other small talk.

The old priest knew she had something important on her mind, so he patiently waited for his guest to get around to the matter.

Finally, she stopped talking, took a deep breath, swallowed hard, and with tears trickling down her cheeks, whispered; "I'm in love."

Annie expained that while working at the place Father Harold had found for her, she met her childhood sweetheart, who happened to be a devout Catholic.

Soon they were seeing each other daily; even went to church together on Sundays. Tears were flowing down her face as she said her man had proposed.

Annie then asked Father Harold if he'd marry them. It took the crusty priest a few minutes to answer because a lump had swelled in his throat.

As Annie had wished, her wedding was held at St. Jude's church with her priestly friend performing the ceremony.

Throughout the war, Father Harold's health continually deteriorated. Nevertheless, in the autumn of *1944* he made good on a promise he'd made several months earlier.

The project got under way when the old priest heard about two *Dominican Sisters of the Perpetual Rosary* who wanted to establish an interracial contemplative *(prayer meditation)* convent in the south.

Intrigued, he decided to offer his help. The problem was the nuns couldn't come to Alabama because they were in cloister *(seclusion from the world)* in Catonsville, Maryland.

Since it was impossible for them to leave their monastery, in spite of failing health he took a train to meet with them.

After a friendly interview, Father Harold invited the nuns to Marbury. He agreed to provide whatever they needed, including a monastery building.

All he asked in return was they have perpetual adoration of the Blessed Sacrament, as well as perpetual recitation of the Holy Rosary for the needs of the people, and for the sisters and priests serving at the *City of St. Jude*.

On August 28, 1944, Father Harold officiated at the "Ceremony of Enclosure" in which the two Dominican nuns again retired from the world.

Thus, the *Dominican Monastery of St. Jude* began its ministry of prayer, adoration, and reparation *(atonement for the sins of people)* in the Diocese of Mobile.

A year later, *September 2, 1945,* the mightiest struggle mankind had even known ended with the unconditional surrender of Japan.

Although stooped and crippled, Father Harold was still a tough competitor as he hijacked building materials assigned to other projects.

Like an eagle hovering over its nest, everyday he went to the building site of the *St. Jude Educational Institute,* and from his wheelchair supervised the construction.

While involved in the project, a story about Father Harold appeared in *The Catholic World* magazine. Fulton Oursler, a writer and personal friend of the outstanding priest, entitled the article, *"The Beggar of St. Jude."*

Editors of Reader's Digest were impressed by the story, and were given permission to reprint it in the October 1946 edition.

A year later, *St. Jude's Educational Institute* was finally ready. The city could now offer schooling from kindergarten, through elementary *(primary)*, to high school *(secondary)*.

St. Jude Education Institute upon completion in 1947.

It was the only educational facility in all of Montgomery offering adult night courses; particularly for war veterans. Soon nearly 700 ex-servicemen had enrolled under the G.I. bill to earn high school diplomas.

Changes were quickly made to meet demands. When it was determined that a vocational school was needed, the institute's basement was converted to accommodate courses in industrial arts.

The faculty was made up of *Sisters of the Holy Family; Vincentian Sisters of Charity;* several priests of the *Congregation of the Resurrection;* lay teachers; and of course, Father Harold himself.

With St. Jude's educational mission fully operational sixteen hours daily, *The Beggar of St. Jude* was ready to launch into a project he had conceived the day he walked through *Shuffle Alley* thirteen years earlier in 1934; a general hospital.

The maternity death rate of both mothers and newborns had always been extremely high in the Montgomery area. It was common knowledge that proper care, and hospitalization would greatly improve the odds for survival.

St. Jude's Social Center clinic had been doing an exceptional job, but the facility was only equipped to handle outpatient ambulatory cases.

So, Father Harold again turned to his list of benefactors, this time for a-million-and-a-half dollars *(equal to approximately $12-million in mid-1980's money).*

With a new burst of energy, he was mailing out appeal letters, and collecting pledges over the telephone.

Little slipped by the shrewd old priest. He was aware that because of the overcrowded conditions of the nation's hospitals, Congress had approved the *Hill-Burton Act in 1946.*

Under the new law, the federal government had authority to approve grants to help states with the cost of building new hospitals, or enlarging, or modernizing those in existence.

With a basic fund of *$25,000,* Father Harold went to Alabama Senator Lester Hill, co-author of the Hill-Burton Act, to ask for his help.

Impressed by the priest's enthusiasm, the senator used his political clout to obtain a grant of a half-a-million dollars for construction of a *165* bed general hospital at the *City of St. Jude.*

Although nearly a million dollars short of the amount needed, Father Harold ordered the project put into motion. In a matter of weeks a construction crew was hard at work.

St. Jude General Hospital - opening day, April 29, 1951.

On April 29, 1951, sixteen years after the *St. Jude Catholic Dispensary opened on Holt Street,* thousands toured the huge cross-shaped, three story *St. Jude General Hospital.*

It was a complete facility providing diagnostic, medical and surgical services, as well as a pediatric section for special care to the handicapped, and mentally retarded children.

The Vincentian Sisters of Charity of Perrysville, Pennsylvania took over administration of the only hospital in Alabama accepting patients without regard to race, color, religious preference, or ability to pay.

All services were performed on an integrated basis. In *1951*, St. Jude's was the only hospital in the entire southeastern United States operated by both a black and white professional and administrative staff.

During the next few years several famous people were admitted to the Catholic hospital including:

Dr. Martin Luther King, Jr's wife who gave birth to two of her children in the St. Jude's maternity ward.

The late country music singer-composer Hank Williams was a patient while trying to break his dependency on drugs.

During the 1950's Alabama polio epidemic, St. Jude's provided invaluable medical services to a large percentage of local citizens.

On July 14, 1951, Montgomery's black community held the first testimonial dinner in Father Harold's honor. After the words of praise had been spoken, the elderly priest stood up and said:

"...You are the people I have always wanted to reach..."

At the annual meeting of the John A. Andrew Clinical Society *(April 9, 1952)* Father Harold was presented with a plaque which read in part:

FOR HIS UNYIELDING FAITH
IN HOPELESS CAUSES

It had taken seventeen years for *The Beggar of St. Jude* to capture the attention of the media. During one of many interviews, a reporter asked Father Harold how the *City of St. Jude* would survive after his passing? In typical fashion he answered:

"I was given up for finished seventeen years ago when I first began St. Jude's Mission.

"Now they say they'll never find another fanatic like me. They're wrong; they'll get all the help they need from St. Jude."

In another interview, the question of fear of failure was raised. In reply the bright eyed priest explained his view on the matter:

"Most people have a fear about beginning projects. I believe that if I begin something I can't finish, someone else may carry it on.

"If I feel that God wants me to start a mission, I am fully confident the means to make it happen will be provided."

But, the old priest was concerned about the future financial needs of the city. As one solution he organized a *St. Jude Mass League* with a primary mission to serve as a perpetual fund raising organization.

The league's secondary mission was to assure the perpetual remembrance of the benefactors in daily Masses. As a group, the membership was to offer regular intercessory prayers for the city's priests, sisters, lay workers, and volunteers.

By 1952, Father Harold had become a sort of local hero, except within his adopted Diocese of Mobile.

In September *('52)* Bishop Toolen honored fifteen of his priests *in recognition of their outstanding contribution to the Church and Her people.*

For reasons which can only be guessed at, Father Harold was not included among those so honored. Being slighted by his own must have hurt, but if it did, nobody ever knew.

A few days later, the old priest moved his office, and living quarters into the west wing of St. Jude's hospital.

During early morning hours when he couldn't sleep, he enjoyed talking with the duty nurses whom he called *"his virgin daughters."*

He was always good for a laugh particularly when making predictions about the future of the city: One of his favorites was about the inside of the church:

> *"After I pass on, some Irish priest will surely place a white marble altar among all the beautiful wood carvings in St. Jude's."*

Father Harold's health weakened, and he became bedridden. His diabetic condition made another operation necessary, this time leaving him paralyzed from the waist down.

Most people would've given up, but not the frail priest of St. Jude. As soon as he was able, he was formulating plans to build a combination *crippled children's hospital and nursing home* for the elderly. He reasoned those beginning life could help those ending it.

When Bishop Toolen heard what Father Harold was planning, he ordered him to stop. The directive acted like a shot of adrenaline, and nobody was surprised when the old priest insisted upon having the tubes providing life support removed.

Against doctor's orders, Father Harold checked out of the hospital in search of a site for *St. Jude's Crippled Children's Hospital and Nursing Home.*

He traveled by train, and automobile, to Tuscaloosa, Alabama, Florida, Tennessee's Lookout Mountain, and to other southern communities. While on the road he suffered a mild stroke which he termed an *annoyance* because it slowed him down.

After returning to St. Jude's, the 71 year old priest checked himself back into the hospital. Within a couple of days he asked *Sister Evangelista,* the hospital administrator, to come to his room.

He confided that over the years he'd been putting money aside, and had accumulated a sizable construction fund to finance his latest venture.

Father Harold said he'd never been concerned with failure, but admitted being worried about this project. Pointing to a drawer he told the nun it contained a bank passbook.

Then he asked the sister to promise, that if he died before the project could be completed, she would make sure Bishop Toolen understood the bank account was *conscience money.*

The Bishop was to know the funds were not to be used for anything other than to finance the construction of a *Crippled Children's Hospital and Nursing Home.*

On October 20, 1952, the annual *St. Jude Solemn Novena* began, but for the first time Father Harold was too weak to attend.

Two days later an emergency call went out; the old priest had suffered a severe heart attack, and was dying.

It was a scene right out of a Hollywood motion picture, complete with weeping nuns kneeling in prayer around his hospital room.

As a young priest entered the room he began sobbing. In his gruff manner, Father Harold said; *"Don't you start, I just got the sisters to stop."*

While the prayers for the dying were being chanted, St. Jude's priest received the Sacrament of the *Anointing of the Sick.*

A few moments later, the old, tired man of God looked directly at each of his nuns, and with a slight hand gesture passed away.

Father Harold Purcell's earthly assignment was over. *The City of St. Jude* was debt-free; not a unit had cost the diocese one penny.

A tremendous crowd turned out for the funeral. The eulogy was delivered by *Father Frank Giri,* Father Harold's personal friend, confessor, and confidant.

Before speaking, he looked directly at those who had not given his friend proper recognition during his lifetime, With admiration he said:

"...Father Harold had more than a spark of genius. Because of this he was greatly misunderstood by us who are less gifted.

"We found fault with him for his passionate urge to get things done. He had faults, many of them.

"The wonder is that with his human failings, he could go to God with a record of magnificent achievements in His service.

"...It behooves us to hearken to the warning of our Blessed Lord: 'He that is sinless amongst you, let him cast the first stone'..."

On October 25th, Father Harold was buried in the lawn between St. Jude's Church, and the Social Center. The slab marking his grave is simply inscribed:

REVEREND HAROLD PURCELL, 1881-1952,
MAY HE REST IN PEACE.

EPILOGUE

Father Harold was succeeded as Director of the *City of St. Jude* by *Monsignor John J. Raleigh.*

One of his first acts was to purchase a large white marble altar, and place it among the wood carving inside the church.

Monsignor Raleigh asked Father Harold's benefactors for their support to build a needed rectory, and to help him carry out his predecessor's final wish for a crippled children's hospital.

As the generous Samaritans of St. Jude had done so many times in the past, again they came through with the needed donations. As a result, on Christmas Day 1954, the new *St. Jude Rectory and Parish Office* was dedicated.

Six years after Father Harold's death, early *1958*, a two-story, St. Jude Exceptional Children's Center *(Father Harold Purcell Memorial)* was completed.

Throughout the life of the *Beggar of St. Jude* he never once accepted less than unconditional fulfillment of a goal.

Since the nursing home for the elderly had been excluded from his plan, in all likelihood he would not have been altogether pleased with his memorial.

In 1958, Monsignor Raleigh added a more adequate convent for the sisters who staffed the various facilities of the city.

In October 1961, Monsignor Raleigh died, and was replaced by *Father Paul J. Mullaney (later promoted to Monsignor).*

In January 1962 with the assistance of the *Vincentian Sisters of Charity,* Father Mullaney established the *St. Jude School of Practical Nursing* with classes in the church basement.

A year later, he ordered construction of a cafeteria-gymnasium *(dedicated, the Monsignor John J. Raleigh Memorial).*

Throughout the *mid-1960's,* the growing staff, and expanding activities of the *City of St. Jude* lead to the construction of a new "Administration Building" *(Father Joseph Jacobi Memorial see upcoming chapter).*

In the spring of 1969, due to an increase in medical demands, a new wing was added to the General Hospital.

Monsignor Mullaney, who had served the people of the Cradle of the Confederacy *(Montgomery)* through the violent civil rights era, retired due to serious illness.

Father Patrick C. O'Connor succeeded him in 1970. His first order was to enlarge the *St. Jude Social Center.*

Five years after he had been placed in charge of the city, the first major reversal to its growth occurred.

St. Jude Rectory and Parish Office–Christmas 1954.

Convent–1958

School Gymnasium–Cafeteria, Father Raleigh Memorial – 1963

St. Jude Exceptional Children's Center
Father Harold Purcell Memorial – 1958

Father Harold during his final years in the early 1950's.

For several years St. Jude's hospital had been suffering serious financial problems. In 1975, as a solution, the decision was made to rent the building and all of its facilities to a group of local doctors. *St. Jude's General Hospital* was no more. In its place; the *Fairview Medical Center*.

Two years later, *Father O'Connor* was transferred to Montgomery's St. Peter's Church as pastor *Monsignor William R. James (Father James)*, well known as a retreat master, mission director, and teacher at St. Jude's High School, became the city's fifth, and as of this writing, current director.

Nearly four decades have gone by since Father Harold's death, and as he predicted, his city in honor of St. Jude continues to live on.

Originally the *city of hope and faith* was built to serve the needy black population of Montgomery. However, during the last decade conditions have changed.

Today, the mission of the *City of St. Jude* has been modified to equally serve the needs of both black and white children.

As for the St. Jude Exceptional Children's Center *(Father Harold Purcell Memorial)*, a serious space shortage has caused a long admissions waiting list.

It's unlikely that Father Harold would have tolerated this predicament. Surely, the *Beggar of St. Jude* would go to his list of Samaritans for whatever was needed to add more floors, or to construct a larger building.

Many people say the likes of Father Harold Purcell will never be known again. This may be true. But, then again, who can predict what St. Jude has planned for his city in the future?

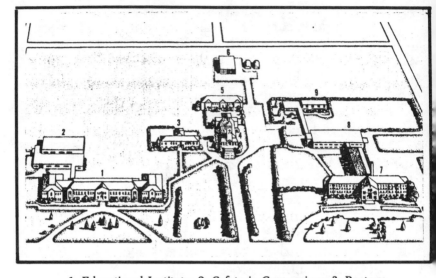

1. Educational Institute; 2. Cafeteria-Gymnasium; 3. Rectory;
4. Church; 5. Social Center; 6. Administration Building;
7. General Hospital; 8. Crippled Children's Hospital; 9.Convent.

ACKNOWLEDGEMENT

The author wishes to acknowledge his indebtedness to Sister Mary Ruth Coffman, O.S.B., author of the book, "Build Me A City" (Pioneer Press), and to the dedicated staff of the City of St. Jude.

Sister Coffman's excellent book offers details about the life of Father Harold and his great work in honor of the "Saint of the Impossible"; the building of his City of St. Jude.

Many of the photographs and much of the information presented would have been lost to history had it not been for Sister Coffman's research..

All wanting to know more about the life of Father Harold Purcell, are encouraged to purchase Sister Mary Ruth Coffman's book, "Build Me A City."

To obtain a copy of this outstanding work send, $5.00 plus $2.00 to cover postage and handling to The City of St. Jude, Montgomery, Alabama, 36196.

CHAPTER IV

ST. JUDE'S WALKING PRIEST

Outstanding people like *Father Harold, and Danny Thomas* are proof that, *one person can make a difference.*

Each, saw what had to be done, established priorities, decided on a course of action, planned a way to achieve the goal, and set about the task of getting the job done.

Both were *positive thinkers* who would not tolerate negativism, and refused to accept defeat. Their unshakable religious faith is what Jesus meant when He said:

> "...I promise you, if you have faith, and do not hesitate, you will be able to do more than I have done. "...If you say to this mountain, remove and be cast into the sea, it will come about. If you will only believe, every gift you ask for in your prayers will be granted..." (Mt 21:21-22).

The story of the *City of St. Jude* would not be complete without a short biography of another special person, *St. Jude's Walking Priest.*

Our subject was born on *March 13, 1897,* during the horse-and-buggy days of the gay *90's,* and was baptized "William Joseph Jacobi." Since his father's name was also William, to avoid confusion he was called by his middle name.

Joseph grew up on a farm in a southern Indiana village, a half mile north of the crossroad town of Bradford. His was a close family in which Catholicism played an important part of everyday life.

From the age of six, when asked what he wanted to be when he grew up, Joseph's answer was always; *"I'm going to be a priest."*

At the age of thirteen, *(Sept 1910)*, he entered St. Meinrad Minor Seminary in southern Indiana; under the Benedictine Fathers.

Determined to become a priest, he struggled through two-and-a-half years of intense study. Upon successful completion, he was transferred to St. Mary's College, in Kentucky under the direction of the *Fathers of the Congregation of the Resurrection.*

Three years later, *(June 1916)*, the nineteen year old farm boy from Indiana graduated from St. Mary's. That autumn, Joseph was assigned to Kitchener, Ontario, Canada where he entered St. Jerome's Novitiate of the Resurrection Fathers *(living quarters and training for those studying for their first vows)*.

Twelve days before Joseph's 21st birthday, *(Mar 1, 1918)*, as a candidate for the priesthood, he took his temporary vows of poverty, chastity, and obedience.

After a short six months assignment at the Resurrectionist Seminary in Chicago, in September 1918 he was off to St. John Cantius Seminary in Missouri, and St. Louis University for advanced study of major seminary courses.

Two years later, he was surprised when transferred to the prestigious international *Gregorian University*, in Rome for advanced studies in theology, and social sciences.

It was a choice assignment to be where the rector was appointed by the pope, and most of the professors were Jesuits from all parts of the world.

As of this writing, among the graduates of the Gregorian University are: 19 saints, 60 popes, and 24 persons who have been beatified.

While Joseph was studying in the *Eternal City,* events of momentous political significance were shaping much of Europe.

Adolph Hitler was leading the organization of the NAZI Party *(Nationalsozialistiche Deutsche Arbeiterpartei).* And in Italy, Benito Mussolini was forming the National Fascist Party.

On St. Jude's feast day, *October 28, 1922,* Joseph stood among the spectators who watched Mussolini march into Rome to transform Italy into a Fascist dictatorship.

It was the same year *Pope Benedict XV* died, and was replaced by *Pope Pius XI* who was an outspoken opponent of Communism, Fascism, and the racial and religious persecutions of Naziism.

However, Joseph was too busy with his studies to be concerned with world events. On *August 10, 1924,* atop Mentorella in the rugged Appenine mountain range in Italy, Joseph was ordained into the priesthood as Father Joseph Jacobi of the Congregation of the Resurrection.

He continued with his studies in Rome for another year, and was privileged to witness several beatifications, and canonizations.

The first was *St. Teresa of Lisieux, the Little Flower of Jesus.* He also participated in the beatification of Blessed Robert Bellarmine *(canonized in 1930).*

St. Therese of the Child of Jesus; The Little
Flower of Jesus. Photo (right) June 7, 1879.

In the fall of *1925* the young priest returned home to the St. John Cantius Congregation of the Resurrection Seminary in St. Louis.

For the next eleven years he served as vice-rector; rector and superior; professor in philosophy, and theology; instructor in Gregorian chant, and other sacred music.

In 1935, the Catholic magazine *Cantian* went into publication, giving the sensitive priest a means through which he could express his innermost feelings. He became a regular contributor of prose and verse, sometimes under an assumed name.

A year later, Father Jacobi was reassigned, to a new seminary associated with the Catholic University in Washington D.C. In the summer of '38, he was ordered back to Rome as Master of Novices at the Resurrection novitiate.

On route to the city of Emperors, Popes, martyrs, and the catacombs, he found himself in Naples, Italy on the feast day *(Sept 19, 1938)* of St. Januarius *(Gennaro)*.

He'd always been fascinated by the story of the two vials of the saint's dried blood which every so often, mysteriously liquified on his feast date.

That afternoon, in the chapel of the *Cathedral of San Gennaro* where the saint's body is enshrined, Father Jacobi was among the privileged to witness the rare miraculous event.

When he took up his duties in Rome, Europe was about to explode into war. Four years earlier, *(1934)*, Hitler's army had marched into Austria.

Since *October 3, 1935,* Italy had been almost continuously at war as Mussolini's fascist military troops had swept through peaceful Ethiopia.

On August 23, 1939, Joseph Stalin, one of the cruelest rulers in history, signed a nonaggression pact with Hitler.

The world stage was set, and at dawn on *September 1, 1939,* German troops invaded Poland. Within two days, Great Britain, and France responded with a declaration of war on Germany.

Not sure Hitler could win, Mussolini held Italy out of the war until *June 10, 1940,* about two weeks before France fell to Germany.

Germany, and Italy declared war on the United States on *December 11, 1941,* four days following Japan's surprise raid on Pearl Harbor, Hawaii.

Italy wasn't militarily or economically prepared for all out warfare. Mussolini's campaigns went

poorly, and most of the nation's food and fuel supplies were channeled to the war effort.

The Italian people were without heating fuel, and
hunger was an everyday condition. About these
trying times, Father Jacobi wrote:

> *"While it was not pleasant to be in an en-
> emy country during war, the Italians did not
> make it unpleasant.*
>
> *"At heart, Italians generally neither had,
> nor displayed any hatred, nor demonstrated
> any ill will toward Americans.*
>
> *"Rather there was a deep feeling of regret
> over war with the United States. In daily life
> we moved about as free and unmolested as
> Italians.*
>
> *"Food shortage, rationing, and starvation
> diets, took the joy out of life, and put all un-
> der nervous tension."*

Father Jacobi could not withstand acute malnutrition. His body swelled, and festering sores developed which would not heal.

Concerned about his health, Father Jacobi's
superior ordered him back to the United States.
The diplomatic service arranged the evacuation.

On *May 31, 1942,* Father Jacobi's ship arrived
safely in New York. Within a few hours he received
the sad news of his father's death, less than six
months earlier.

At the same time he was told about his next assignment as a missionary working among the Negroes in Pensacola, Florida.

It took only a few weeks of his mother's home
cooking for his open sores to heal. As much as he

enjoyed being with his family, he was anxious to get on with his missionary work. About this he wrote:

> *"Mission endeavor is that of a priest who has boundless love for his people, a real father's love as towards a family of countless children.*
>
> *"It's work which requires activity without limit, perpetual motion, enterprise and resourcefulness; an outlook towards unceasing expansion.*
>
> *"Lacking the like qualifications, a priest had best not be sent to a mission field. But once a priest is steeped in mission work he can hardly divorce his soul from it again."*

When Father Jacobi arrived in Pensacola in *July 1942,* to his surprise, he found no existing mission; not even a building from which to work, or live. Nevertheless, it was his responsibility to establish a mission house, so he set to work.

By August, he had located a vacant two car garage near Pensacola, along the Lillian Highway *(U.S. 98)* on Perdido Bay. At his request the building was purchased for his headquarters.

At first few calls were received from local parishes, or nearby military camps, but as the months passed, matters improved, and he was once again an active priest.

Father Jacobi had definite feelings about missionary work, of which he wrote:

> *"I had loved all my priestly assignments since my departure from the seminary in 1925. But, from my first entry into the new field, my*

soul had inseparably wedded itself to mission life."

The priest was deeply engrossed in his new found love when a call requesting long term assistance went out to the Resurrectionist missionaries from *Father Harold Purcell.*

Without a word of complaint, in *March 1943,* Father Jacobi moved to the *City of St. Jude.* He was followed by two other Resurrectionists: Father Anthony Gozdziak who was placed in charge of the Holy Ghost Catholic Mission in Marbury, Alabama; and Father Casimir Wlezien, who became Father Harold's personal assistant.

Father Jacobi's observations about the assignment as recorded in his autobiography:

> *"Father Harold Purcell was solely the head of the Montgomery Institution including being pastor of the developing parish of St. Jude.*
> *"However, because of his age, infirmities, and many preoccupations, he was not able to work effectively in the mission, and pastoral cares. He was, however, very able to manage the business of St. Jude's entire enterprise.*
> *"So, he told me, 'You are the pastor. Whatever you say goes in the parish.'"*

With the assignment of more *Resurrectionists,* Father Harold purchased a vacant school on the north side of the city, in the center of the railroad, stock, lumber, and junk yards.

It was a miserable, and notoriously violent section of Montgomery with a well earned reputation of *the bucket of blood* district. Father Harold named his newest venture, the *Nazareth Catholic Mission.*

Resurrectionists Father Stephen Juda, and Brother Matthew, were given the job of setting up the mission. Under their guidance things progressed rapidly, and by fall *('43),* THE NAZARETH CATHOLIC MISSION PAROCHIAL SCHOOL was ready for enrollment.

Two *Sisters of the Holy Family of Nazareth* were reassigned from the *City of St. Jude* to teach in the new daughter mission.

Meanwhile, Father Jacobi had settled in as pastor of St. Jude's church. He took care of the daily Masses, and the two on Sundays, *(one for adults;the other for children).* He also taught religious instructions.

The dedicated missionary found the job as pastor of St. Jude's a difficult assignment. Nobody came to the rectory, or telephoned about pastoral matters. He reasoned that if the people wouldn't come to him, he'd just have to reach out to them. About this he wrote:

> *"When I was back in St. Louis I liked to take my walks in the streets where colored people lived. I could at least say to many I met; 'How-do-you-do?' Now and then I could talk a little with some. It gave me considerable familiarity with colored people."*

From then on, Father Jacobi spent most of his time walking among the black population in the vicinity of St. Jude's; through streets, alleys, lanes, and hill paths of gravel, clay, and mud.

He went into sections where the people lived in extreme poverty. He got to know the elderly, the sick, and others who had suffered misfortune, or abandonment without hope.

Through St. Jude's rummage he provided some immediate relief. He sent food to the hungry, milk to babies, necessities to the sick, clothing and fuel to as many of the needy as possible. In extreme cases he demanded the County Welfare Department take action.

At Father Jacobi's disposal was the use of an automobile, but he refused it. When asked why, he replied:

> *"The auto would certainly make things easier, but when I walk through neighborhoods I see and visit practically everybody. For people to see the car pass and remark, 'There goes Father,' means very little to anyone.*
>
> *"On foot I can salute everybody, say a passing word to many, pause a moment, and have a few words at door steps; inquire about possible neighborhood sick, and above all see the children and get to know them all.*
>
> *"By walking, I'm part of the neighborhood. This means immensely more to the people, and to me as pastor of a church where there are hundreds of black non-Catholics for every Catholic."*

In time, Father Jacobi was being called *St. Jude's Walking Priest*. Everybody knew he had a special love for children. Whenever the youngsters saw the tall man in the black robe, they'd shout, *"Here come Fah!"*

Excitedly they'd run to meet him, the fastest would get to hold his hand for a while. The rest were happy just to walk along at his side, chattering away about this and that. He wrote of this experience:

"There's no love or devotion like that of a child's heart, and these were precious to me! They were poor, shabby and seemingly neglected, but always most precious and devoted.

"I called them my little 'good-for-nothings, precious good-for-nothings', knowing how dear they were to God. How many children did I see sick, sometimes dying, or bewildered at the bedside of a parent who had died!"

St. Jude's Walking Priest made it a point to ask about the sick, because he knew the importance of a visit. Whenever necessary, he'd take the sister in charge of the clinic with him to help, or get a city doctor to make a house call.

There were two hospitals within a few miles of St. Jude's which served the medical needs of the black population. Everyday he'd visit both; when possible a couple of times.

On the other side of Montgomery were two other hospitals which accepted black patients, plus the County Sanitarium for those suffering with tuberculosis.

He stopped at every bed with a jovial remark, a word of spiritual encouragement, or an *Our Father*. When meeting patients in critical condition special words of prayer were offered.

Officially, Father Jacobi was pastor of St. Jude's church, however, he usually found himself in the role of visiting nurse, doctor, or social worker. But, more importantly, he was the neighborhood priest.

When a sick, elderly, or disabled person wanted to become Catholic, he'd make time to sit by their bedsides to help with the necessary religious instructions.

He carried Communion out to the sick. At first those receiving were few, but with time the numbers steadily increased.

All the while *St. Jude's Walking Priest* was serving the sick of Montgomery, he was suffering from cancer of the neck. He wrote:

> *"My one regret is that I lost many months of my work during the last years I was at St. Jude's by long, repeated absences in St. Louis for doctor's care and treatments."*

In spite of his terminal condition, for a decade Father Jacobi brought comfort to those in *desperate, and seemingly hopeless situations.* He was a true friend, listener, and supporter to all who needed help.

During the ten years of his walking ministry, baptisms at St. Jude's increased. Father Harold appreciated his pastor's important contribution to the parish. On more than one occasion, the tough old priest publicly stated that Father Jacobi's walking missionary was:

> *"The Gift of God to the City of St. Jude. I built the church, my friend brought the congregation."*

A year after Father Harold's death on October 22, 1952, *St. Jude's Walking Priest* was reassigned to the Resurrection Catholic Center, formerly the *Nazareth Catholic Mission.*

For more than two years he carried on with his walking ministry, all the while suffering agonizing pain from an open cancerous lesion on his neck.

The final chapter in the inspiring biography of *St. Jude's Walking Priest* has to do with the last six years of his active ministry.

In March 1955, Father Jacobi moved to Dothan, a thriving little city in the southeastern corner of Alabama, bordering Florida and Georgia. There he rented a vacant building on the west side of Dothan where he planned to open a kindergarten for black children.

Even though the authorities at City Hall had given verbal permission to proceed, he encountered annoying opposition from the white population, as well as from the local Chief of Police. Fearing trouble, the Mayor asked Father Jacobi to look for another location. He recorded in his autobiography:

> *"I did not go to Dothan to start trouble, but to do good. So I dropped the kindergarten for the time being, and began looking for another place."*

There were approximately 10,000 black people living within the city, with many more in the surrounding suburbs. As for black Catholics, they were exceedingly rare throughout all of southeastern Alabama; in Dothan they were just about non-existent. Father Jacobi wrote about asking a woman if she knew any black Catholics:

> *"No, and ya ain't goin' to find colored Catholics in Dothan. We're all Baptists and Methodists. The Catholic Church ain't never been open to us."*

Meanwhile, Father Jacobi continued his walking missionary ministry which bothered some of the leading citizens. He was harassed by the police in his living quarters, and stopped for questioning while on his rounds.

Nobody was going to run him out of the city. He complained to the Police Commissioner; when that failed, he took his case to the Mayor who saw to it he was never bothered again.

It was the fall of *1956* before Father Jacobi located a building for his kindergarten and day nursery on the east side of the city.

This time he obtained an Alabama license officially authorizing him to go into business. When everything was ready he put up a sign:

RESURRECTION CATHOLIC CENTER-CHAPEL,
DAY NURSERY AND KINDERGARTEN

During Father Jacobi's half dozen years in Dothan, he worked without an assistant priest, brother, or nun.

His only helpers were a few women he hired to teach in the kindergarten, and to care for the youngsters in the nursery.

Everyday, approximately forty children were fed a morning and afternoon snack, and a properly balanced hot lunch. His unpublished autobiography describes his inner feelings:

> *"Every day at the nursery is a big day. A big day for the children and a big day for the instructors, and myself. As for myself, I am the happiest man in the world with this work.*
>
> *"But I still had to get out among the people, visit the sick in the hospitals, and carry forward the formation of our little parish.*

"The loss of my voice to a great extent has become a formidable handicap.   My doctor advised me I had to rest if I wanted to live. Activity, not rest is what builds a mission."

On October 31, 1961, failing health forced his return to St. Louis. He wrote:

"...I'm under the doctor's care, inactive and unable to return to my beloved field of missionary work."

On *June 6, 1965,* cancer took the life of Father Joseph Jacobi, *St. Jude's Walking Priest.*

EPILOGUE

The legacy Father Jacobi left to the people of the "City of St. Jude" and Dothan, Alabama can never be fully evaluated.

City of St. Jude Administration Building
Father Jacobi Memorial - 1966

However, official reports filed by local elementary school teachers were in agreement that the children from the *Resurrection Catholic Day Nursery and Kindergarten* were far ahead of others who had not enjoyed a similar advantage.

When he became pastor of St. Jude's there were only a few Catholic families in the parish; today there are *350*.

St. Jude's Walking Priest
Father, Joseph Jacobi. C.R., 1910-1965

Eighteen months after the Resurrectionist missionary's death, in tribute to his devotion to the poor, and sick of the parish, the *City of St. Jude*

Administration Building was dedicated, The Father Joseph Jacobi Memorial.

Even after more than three decades, whenever the name of "St. Jude's Walking Priest" is mentioned to anyone who knew him, a gentle smile is followed by the testimony: "*He's a saint!*"

CHAPTER V

LITTLEST ANGEL

We often hear the phrase; *"Life is filled with crosses to bear."* Certainly, no sensible person would quarrel with the statement, for experience teaches that regardless of status all manner of things happen to everyone of us; no person escapes.

Yet, when something goes amiss, how often God is blamed! One of the best sermons on suffering, and faith this author has ever heard was spoken by Air Force Reserve Chaplain, Captain, William J. Hamilton *(Father Bill):*

"This has been a week of wecks; *Monday,* my father suffered a stroke. His doctor, a close family friend, told us his only chance was immediate surgery. Carefully, he explained the slim odds my father had of surviving the operation.

"While trying to deal with this situation, the following day, *Tuesday,* the surgeon's *21* year old son was killed in a fiery car crash. I loved the boy like a brother, and his death was a shock.

"The next day, *Wednesday,* my mother's sister died from cancer. I couldn't understand why all this was happening me, and I placed the blame squarely on my *Boss.* Why was God picking on me? Throughout the night I prayed for an answer.

"Thursday morning, while awaiting news about the outcome of my father's operation,

my prayers were suddenly answered. I wasn't being punished; everything that had happened was perfectly normal.

"My father was old, had suffered several heart attacks, and was under doctor's care for years. His stroke should not have been a surprise.

"The police report about the surgeon's son revealed he had been driving at a high rate of speed, lost control of his car, and slammed into a tree. Any experienced insurance investigator will testify that youth tends to speed.

"Then there was my aunt's passing. The poor woman had been suffering with terminal cancer for months. Instead of anger, I should have been thankful because her death was a blessing.

"God answered my prayers by giving me the *insight* to understand the truth."

This chapter is directed to all who know someone, or are themselves suffering the *loss of religious faith*. Nearly every family of every religious persuasion has experienced this kind of disappointment.

Young people have always questioned the values of parents. All too often one of the first casualties is the family religion. Fortunately, with maturity comes a degree of *wisdom,* and a fair percentage who strayed from the family religion eventually return of their own accord.

But, what about those who have cast off their religious roots, and need help to return? We've been taught that since every person is given a free will, the Lord will not intervene unless asked through prayer.

Obviously *lost sheep* don't pray, but concerned relatives, and friends sometimes ask patron saints for help with these situations.

What you're about to read is not a typical story. It concerns a young man who not only lost his faith, but became an agnostic *(belief that no one can prove there is a God, or a spiritual hereafter)*.

At every opportunity, he'd challenge all comers to religious debates, and took delight in shocking friends with irreverent statements.

This worried his mother, grandmother, and a friend he called a *religious fanatic*. Independently, the trio prayed through St. Jude, and other saints to do something.to enlighten the young man.

However, the circumstances which had to be overcome in order to guide the teenager back to the fold were very complicated. To understand what was involved, it's essential to review the boy's unconventional childhood.

Our subject's real name is *"Jackie:"* Boston, Massachusetts was his place of birth on July 5. When he was born, his mother was not much more than a child herself; sixteen years old.

Even though his father was twenty-four, he was immature; most certainly not ready to accept the obligations of parenthood. Like most everything in the man's life, he was a less than successful floor wax salesperson who took to running away, rather than facing up to his responsibilities.

Shortly before Jackie's second birthday, his father secretly sold the household furniture to a second hand dealer. With the few dollars the sale brought, he abandoned his wife, and son.

The divorce hearing was stormy, and when the dust had settled, custody of the boy was awarded to his mother. A modest monthly child support was ordered by the judge, and visitation privileges spelled out.

As happens in too many divorce cases, Jackie became a pawn in the post divorce relationship. After a few turbulent visits, his father never returned; soon the support checks stopped.

Not knowing what to do, Jackie's mother asked her ex-husband's family to speak to the man about his neglect of financial duty. When they refused to get involved, the father's family branch was permanently eliminated from the boy's life.

A warrant was issued for the delinquent man's arrest. When hauled into court, the judge sentenced him to six months in the *House of Correction* at Deer Island, Massachusetts. A few days after his release, with indifference for his son's well-being, the man headed for parts unknown.

Jackie's mother began to worry and became paranoid. She was convinced the *Child Welfare Department,* or her ex-husband were waiting to take her son away from her on the grounds she was unable to provide proper support.

Without financial help the frightened, bitter teenager found herself the sole bread winner, and eventually she turned into a workaholic waitress.

Six days a week, she'd arrive at the restaurant in time for the breakfast rush. After a nap on the ladies room couch, she'd be up and ready to work both the lunch, and dinner meals.

The hours were many, the work hard, and at night she was exhausted. Once home, in minutes she'd drop off into a sound sleep. Needless to point out, her social life amounted to zero.

Jackie's roots were firmly planted in Somerville, Massachusetts, a heavily populated, manufacturing, and residential city, about three miles northwest of downtown Boston. The neighborhood was made up primarily of Italian, Portuguese, English, and Irish Catholic families.

Like the other rough cities adjacent to Boston, the children of Somerville were divided into street gangs. Jackie was a member of the *Beacon Street Gang*.

The unified structure of the group turned out to be extremely important in his development, because his family, on his mother's side, was not particularly close-knit.

For six years the whereabouts of the boy's father remained a mystery. Then, in *1942* came word the man had been drafted into the Army. Child support, in the form of government allotment checks began arriving monthly.

Never anything else, not a telephone call, or a birthday card, or a Christmas present. Gang members bragged about their fathers and brothers who were away fighting the war. But, Jackie knew nothing about his father, so he made up tales about the man's heroic military adventures.

Needs of the nation took Jackie's mother out of the restaurant, and put her into the factory. With lunch pail in hand she went off to manufacture tanks in the Somerville Ford Motor Company assembly plant. The job offered plenty of overtime, and the boy continued to be more or less in charge of his own destiny.

When Jackie was in the second grade, he didn't like school, so he quit. For three months he was an elementary school dropout.

His daily routine was to get out of bed whenever he pleased, take money from the bowl where his mother kept change, buy candy, soda, comic books, junk, and go to matinee movies.

Whenever a member of his gang stayed home from school because of illness, for company and to pass the day away Jackie would visit. Since most of the parents were away at work, few knew what was going on.

With too much free time, Jackie drifted into shoplifting. Every couple of days, he'd go into the five and ten cent store in Cambridge, and steal things. It was easy, and before long he became careless. He'd just stuff whatever he wanted into his pockets, and leave the store.

One afternoon while on a spree, the store manager grabbed hold of the young shoplifter, and ordered him to empty his pockets. Out came an assortment of toys, and trinkets.

When the manager let go of his captive's arm, Jackie took the opportunity to make his escape. With the manager in pursuit, he darted between the customers legs, and out the door to a successful getaway. The experience was terrifying, but it brought his career in crime to an abrupt end.

Several mornings later, the doorbell rang at Jackie's flat. When he peeked out between the curtains, he was shocked to see *Mr. Ireland,* the truant officer. He'll always remember hearing the pounding of his heart as he stood perfectly motionless waiting for the man to leave.

Since Jackie was not accustomed to being held accountable for his actions, within a few hours he dismissed the incident. That afternoon he went to the movies, and after school hours, joined the gang to play football.

Regardless of who was winning, around six o'clock the game ended because his friends were called home for dinner. With nothing to do, Jackie wandered home, opened and heated a can of something or other, and downed a quart of milk.

Later the gang regrouped by the corner store, and talked until about nine o'clock. One at a time, the call came to go home, and only after the last had left, did Jackie do the same.

That night as he opened the door, Jackie saw his mother's swollen eyes, and immediately recalled *Mr. Ireland's* visit. Without asking for an explanation, with wire coat hanger in hand, again and again she whipped him on the upper thighs.

The following morning, instead of going to work, she escorted her son to the school principal. For the remainder of the year, Jackie's second grade teacher tried to please him. In June, even though failing, she promoted him to the third grade with a *"B"* report card.

Throughout the summer vacation Jackie's mother worried about his skipping classes in the upcoming fall. As a precautionary measure, she had him transferred to a school near her sister's apartment in the Allston section of Boston.

Every morning, along with the workers, the young boy took a twenty minute *Boston Elevated* bus trip through Harvard Square, Cambridge to Allston, on the other side of the Charles River.

Before going to school he reported to his aunt. At lunch time it was back to her apartment for a small bowl of Lipton Noodle Soup, and a glass of cold milk. Except for vacations, and weekends the menu never varied. At the end of each school day before returning to Somerville, he made a final report.

The third grade teacher knew about his truancy record, and overcompensated with excessive pampering. She conveniently looked the other way when he cheated. When the school year ended, as before, he was a failing student. Nevertheless, she promoted him with an *"A"* report card.

Throughout the summer school vacation Jackie pleaded with his mother to transfer him back to the Somerville school system. After making every conceivable promise, the poor woman surrendered.

Two months into the fourth grade, X-rays confirmed that Jackie's appendix was about to rupture. An emergency appendectomy was performed, followed by two weeks of hospitalization, and a couple of months of home convalescence. By the time Jackie got back to school he was so far behind, there was no possible way of catching up.

In June the boy's free pass ended. No matter what he said, or how many tears he shed, the teacher refused to promote him. Most of his gang went on to the next higher elementary school which was on the other side of the city.

Repeating the fourth grade with younger children was degrading. Not being able to walk to and from school with his gang, or take part in their extracurricular activities made Jackie feel like an outsider. There was no way to get around this teacher, so he buckled down to his studies, and was legitimately promoted.

During the spring and fall of *1945,* World War II was winding down. Germany had surrendered on *May 7th,* and before school resumed, on *September 2nd,* Japan signed final peace terms.

With the veterans returning home, the women were no longer needed in the factories, and Jackie's mother went back to waitress work. Like millions of others, his father was honorably discharged, and quickly vanished along with the monthly support checks.

Religion was important in Jackie's development even though going to church didn't seem to match the youngster's profile. His mother, and grandmother *(who lived in Arlington, Massachusetts)* were devout Catholics. Both honored St. Anthony, complete with home altars, and vigil candles.

They were also devotees of St. Jude, long before most people had even heard of him. Not a day passed without the two women offering prayers through their patron saints to guide, and protect the boy.

Every Lenten season, Jackie and his mother attended the annual St. Francis Xavier *Novena of Grace* at St. Joseph's parish in Somerville. The undisciplined youth attended catechism classes, received First Holy Communion, Confirmation, and rarely missed Sunday Mass, or Holy Days. Yet, all who knew the youngster would never describe him as a religious type.

In his high school sophomore year Jackie's grandmother bought him, *for fifty dollars,* a mint condition 1937 Oldsmobile coupe. The squealing of tires only added to his reputation as the *wild one.*

When Jackie was sixteen years old, he stood six feet tall, weighed a little over a hundred pounds, had dark circles under his eyes from *chronic sinus,* and was plagued with *asthma.*

He didn't like discipline, and hated school. At the conclusion of his Junior year in *June 1952,* when he failed one subject, he used it as an excuse to become a high school dropout.

The unrestrained juvenile tried a few jobs, but didn't like work anymore than school. His mother, and grandmother kept him in spending money, so he bummed around. Life was a series of late night dates, and sleeping till afternoon.

A couple of years earlier, the United States had become involved in another war, when on *June 27, 1950,* President Truman ordered military forces to help defcnd South Korea.

During the early *'50's,* gang members began going their separate ways and the group was slowly breaking up. Most entered the labor market, a few went off to college, others enlisted in the navy, marines, or coast guard.

Jackie wasn't particularly patriotic, but he had a strong desire to join the Air Force. He tried to persuade friends to enlist with him rather than to take the chance of being drafted into the Army.

On the evening of the *fourth of July, 1952,* one of the gang decided to go along and join the Air Force. Since Jackie had always done whatever he wanted, whenever he wanted, without guidance, or counsel, he signed on the dotted line.

During the induction physical examination, the doctor easily identified the *sinus, and asthma* conditions. When asked why Jackie hadn't noted his problems on the medical questionnaire form, the boy denied having any such symptoms..

For some reason, which will never be understood, the doctor allowed the sickly youth to pass. A few hours later Jackie was standing in a group with his right hand raised; taking the military oath. Within hours he was on a train bound for *Sampson Air Base* in upper New York state.

It took less than an hour of basic training for Jackie to realize, he'd made a *serious error.* Military discipline was not for him. All he wanted was to get back to civilian life, and as quickly as possible.

A couple of mornings later, his flight *(basic training unit)* was marched to the base hospital for a follow-up physical examination. He was overjoyed for surely when the doctors got a look at his medical conditions, it would be back to Somerville, the Oldsmobile, and a life of fun and games.

With anticipation, he wrote on the medical questionnaire, in large bold letters: *"SUFFERS FROM ASTHMA, AND CHRONIC SINUS."* However, when examined, the doctor couldn't find any trace of either condition. The young Airman's lungs were free of wheezing, his sinuses clear, and the inside of his nasal passage a healthy pink.

Like it or not, civilian life was a thing of the past; at least for the next four years. Throughout the months of basic training, and technical school Jackie fought the system. It wasn't until his first active duty assignment at *Sewart Air Force Base,* near Nashville, Tennessee, did he begin accepting military life.

At the same time his religious faith started fading. Before long he was no longer attending Mass. When his mother, and grandmother learned about his loss of faith, rows of vigil candles were set ablaze. They called on their patron saints to keep him out of harms reach, and help him find the route back to his religion.

Military forces were in the second year of involvement in the Korean Conflict. A number of Jackie's Air Force buddies had been shipped to the combat zone. However, when his number came up for overseas assignment, instead of the Far East, he was ordered to England.

Within a short time he met a British girl, got married, and became a teenage father of a baby girl. Jackie, or *John* as he now wanted to be called, formed an unlikely friendship with a burly Irishman named *Charlie Hannon.* They had nothing in common except the same military unit.

Charlie was 40 years old, loved the Air Force, and Catholic to the point of fanaticism. He even lived with his wife, and two young children in a priest's home a few miles from the air base *(RAF Station Sculthorpe)*.

Every evening following dinner, the Hannons dropped to their knees, and as a family recited the Rosary. This daily ritual was never interrupted even when John was visiting. *An interesting side note is, St. Jude was also one of the Hannon's patron saints.*

Every time the two men got together, for hours they'd argue about religion, and only stopped when John became blasphemous. Every argument ended the same way; Charlie getting flustered, blessing himself, and saying; *"I'd be afraid to talk about God the way you do!"*

For years Charlie tried to talk John into getting his daughter baptized. More or less to humor the *old guy,* he finally agreed to let the Hannons be his daughter's godparents.

In *1955,* Charlie's England overseas tour was up and he was reassigned to Ramstein Air Base in Germany. Odds of the two families meeting again were astronomical, not only because military friendships are transitory, but their goals were so different.

John was a dedicated civilian who counted off the days to discharge. His plan was to return to Massachusetts to become a state trooper. Charlie was career Air Force, ready for world-wide duty.

In any event, before long the Hannons were forgotten. Then, something unexplainable happened; John's feeling changed about military life, and he reenlisted for six more years. The Air Force had become his career objective, and for the first time John had purpose, and direction.

In *1956,* as his overseas assignment in England was drawing to an end, John was selected *"Outstanding Airman"* for all of Europe. He enjoyed the experience of living in foreign countries, so instead of returning to the United States, he volunteered for a second consecutive overseas tour of duty.

John was pleased when informed his new assignment was *West Germany,* and of all the possible world-wide military installations, it was *Ramstein Air Base.* Friendship with the Hannons took up where it left off, and the old argument about religion resumed anew.

On *June 8, 1958,* John's wife gave birth to a beautiful, healthy girl, *"Debbie."* Christmas week in Germany was a happy time. All seemed just about perfect. John came home from the base with a small tree, and his oldest daughter, now four years old, helped with the decorations.

Three days before Christmas, Debbie woke up with a cough, and fever. The Air Force doctor who examined her assured John she had nothing more serious than a bad cold.

But, his diagnosis was not correct, for sometime during the early morning hours, Debbie died in her sleep; without benefit of baptism. The autopsy report read:

"Acute Trachoebronchitis, Bronchopheumona, Generalized Etiology undetermined."

John's controlled world fell into pieces. The Hannons tried to help, but the pain, and feelings of absolute helplessness were unbearable.

A child's death is always a shattering blow no matter when, or how it happens. But, imagine how much greater the impact at Christmas time with the absent baby's unopened presents in place under the tree as if at any moment you'll wake up, and the nightmare will be over.

On Christmas Eve, *Cardinal Francis Spellman,* the apostolic vicar to the United States Armed Forces happened to be visiting Ramstein Air Base on his annual overseas military Christmas tour.

John wanted to speak with him. After a lengthy conversation he asked the Cardinal for his intercessory prayers to help during this most painful of times.

Christmas morning, John's religious faith was miraculously restored as he, and his family went to Mass in the base chapel.

There's one more fact that should be known about John; he's the author of this book; *John Wallace Spencer.*

EPILOGUE

Looking back, the author understands that due to his unorthodox childhood, youthful age, carefree devil-may-care personality, and can-do anything attitude, something powerful had to be done to get his attention.

He wasn't praying himself, but his mother, grandmother, and the Hannons were through St. Anthony, St. Jude, and other saints.

As for being a pious man, John maintains he's not in the same league as his mother, grandmother, or the Hannons. Like Danny Thomas, he's simply a man who has faith in Jesus, and St. Jude.

During his second Air Force enlistment, the author attended night school to earn his high school diploma. He furthered his education by taking courses at the University of Maryland, and Westfield State College in Massachusetts.

Upon completion of more than ten years of Air Force active duty, John was honorably discharged, and returned to civilian life. As a result of schooling, training, and experience received courtesy of his assignment with the *Armed Forces Radio and Television Service,* the author entered the commercial broadcasting industry.

As of this writing, he's still associated with the military as an active member of the *United States Air Force Reserve.*

Concerning his amazing recovery from *asthma* and *chronic sinus,* without the advantage of personal diagnosis, the consistent theory among physicians is; the asthma and sinus conditions were psychosomatic *(medical disorders created by the mind or emotions).*

However, on the other hand, most of those questioned are willing to concede that if the described symptoms were real, it would indeed take a miracle to bring about an overnight cure. Nonetheless, neither medical problem has ever returned.

During the author's military assignment in England, his *mother* remarried, and is happily retired in Florida. His *grandmother* suffered a severe paralytic stroke in *1979,* and is permanently confined to a Cambridge hospital.

Charlie Hannon, the all important antagonist, died suddenly in *1965* of a heart attack on a Texas Air Force Base.

As for the author's children, his daughter who was born in England, graduated from Northeastern University as a certified physical therapist. She lives with her husband, and baby son in a suburban Boston city.

Twin boys were born to the Spencers in *1964*. In the near future they'll both be graduating from a New England university as computer scientists.

The pain of Debbie's death has been gone for many years, but there will always be the lingering question of what might have been?

Whenever the author meets young people who have misplaced their religious faith, he can't help but wonder if relatives, and friends are praying for them through patron saints. He also wonders if they'll return to their religion on their own, or will strong measures be necessary to bring them back?

Strange that a young man who lacked discipline, and purpose became an author, an occupation requiring total discipline. Then again, considering the subject of this book, perhaps *it's not so strange!*

The following poem, about the passing of a child, was composed by Ben Burroughs of the Chicago Herald-American. It appeared in *Sketches,* and in *Leaves*.

WHEN GOD CALLS LITTLE CHILDREN

When God calls little children to dwell with Him above,
We mortals always question the wisdom of His love.
For no heartache compares with the death of one small child.
Who does so much to make this world seem wonderful and mild.
Perhaps God tires always calling the aged to His fold,
And so He picks a rosebud before it can grow old.

God knows how much we need them, and so He
takes but few,
To make the land of heaven more beautiful to view.
Believing this is difficult, but somehow we must try:
The saddest word that man can know will always be
"good-bye."
And so when little ones depart, we who are left
behind,
Must realize how much God loves them, for angels
are hard to find.

CHAPTER VI

CHILDHOOD TO PENTECOST.

It's nearly impossible to meet a person who hasn't heard of St. Jude Thaddeus. Yet, other than being a saint, few know who he is, or anything about his life, or earthly ministry.

Unfortunately, early Christian writers have provided few details about the holy man. Any widespread public recognition of Jude Thaddeus, from his martyrdom in *A.D.* 79 until after *1911* is extremely difficult to trace.

For almost two-thousand years, Jude was a *forgotten saint;* lost to history. However, since he was one of Jesus' original *Twelve Apostles,* devotion never totally faded away.

The void of recorded information about his life, and works caused biblical scholars, historians, scientists, and researchers to diligently sift through scattered fragments of ancient records, early writings, legends, and traditions.

As a result of centuries of painstaking dedication, an acceptable biographical portrait of the saint, who today inspires such great confidence, has been pieced together.

For unknown reasons, during the early *20th century,* affection for St. Jude suddenly began surfacing. His popularity spread so rapidly that in only a few decades he went from near total obscurity to one of the most highly honored of all the saints.

In four generations word of his power as a heavenly mediator has spread throughout much of the *Orient, Armenia, Central and South America, Europe, the United States, Canada, and Mexico.*

One indication of the size of his following came to light through a survey on prayer published in the U.S. Catholic magazine. Figures showed that among 790-million baptized Roman Catholics, St. Jude was second in popularity only to St. Mary, Jesus' Mother.

As for his childhood, like that of Jesus, it remains a mystery. However, ancient documents indicate Jesus, and Jude were about the same age, and their families were closely related. *(App A)*.

We know Jesus worked with His foster father as a carpenter among the humble people in the hillside town of Nazareth in the province of Galilee in northern Palestine *(now a town in the northern most region of Israel). (Lk 2:51).*

Jude's ancestors were of the farming tribe of Judah, and most likely his family lived off the land in a valley village, also in the northern most part of Palestine.

Since the two related Jewish families were close neighbors, it's reasonable to assume that Jude and his brothers were childhood playmates of Jesus. *(Mt 14:55).*

As a matter of record, Jude's entire family is prominently mentioned in connection with Jesus' later public ministry. Jude's mother, *Mary of Alpheus;* his father; and his brothers; Joses *(Joseph),* and Symeon *(Simeon - Simon),* all became important disciples during the Church's early years. Two of Jude's other brothers, James the Less, and Matthew *(Levi),* became Apostles.

The greatest proof Jesus was who He claimed to be, lies in the fact that His friends, and close relatives dedicated their lives to Him; even suffering martyrs deaths.

Early Christian scholar, Bishop John Chrysostom *(A.D. 345-407)* suggested that when Matthew, and

James were young men, they left the farm to become customs tax officers. *(Mk 2:16)*.

Church historian *Eusebius* wrote that, with the exception of John, Jude and the other Apostles, were married. It takes little imagination to see Jesus, His family, and close friends as guests at Jude's wedding feast.

Nothing is known about Jude's wife, or his children, however, *Hegesippus* revealed that several years after Jude's martyrdom, two of his grandsons, Zoker and James, came into prominence. *(More about them in Chapter VIII)*.

Tradition says, Jesus was *19* years old when Joseph died. Jewish custom dictated that widows, and children had to be taken into the homes of relatives. Perhaps Jesus, and His Mother lived with Jude's family for a time.

To understand Jude's role in the missionary development of Christianity, and also for sake of continuity, a portion of the final months of Jesus' earthly life must be reviewed.

At about the age of 30, Jesus moved to the frontier town of *Capernaum* where He began His public ministry. His popularity among the common people grew rapidly, especially with the social outcasts, and enslaved.

Needing helpers, He went to *Bethsaida,* and other towns around the *Sea of Galilee* where He recruited several disciples including Simon and his brother Andrew; John, and his brother James.

Later, along with other disciples, Jude, and his brothers; Matthew *(Levi)*, and James the Less were chosen.

Nothing is known about Jude's selection, in fact, his name is not even mentioned until listed among the Apostles.

For months Jesus traveled in the company of the disciples. One night He went into the mountains to pray for guidance. At dawn He returned, called the disciples together, and appointed twelve to be His Apostles. *(Lk 6.13)*.

At every opportunity, Jesus worked with Jude, and the others in Capernaum, from where they traveled to nearby towns, and villages.

Before touching on the Crucifixion, it should be noted the name "Jew" is never used in this work to describe those who were responsible for Jesus' execution.

Placing the blame on the Jewish nation is a grievous error. For instance, during Jesus' earthly ministry there were about 8-million Jews scattered about the ancient world. Great numbers of Jews lived outside Judea mainly in; Alexandria, Cyrenaica (northern Africa), Rome, Babylon, Antioch (Antakya, Turkey), and Ephesus.

It's also important to keep in mind that Jesus, the Apostles, disciples, and most of the early Christian converts were born, and educated as Jews.

During the first 35 years of the new religion, followers of Jesus' doctrine were thought of as a sect of Judiasm. Even today, Christianity, and Mohammedanism are called the "daughters of Judaism".

Those directly responsible for Jesus' Crucifixion were members of the most active religious-political groups in Judaism; Pharisees, and Sadducees.

TWELVE APOSTLES

Apostle means, "one sent forth, a messenger". The word apostolos is of Greek origin; in Hebrew it's Shaliach. Apostle is reserved for the disciples Jesus personally selected to assist Him with His earthly mission.

Most of the Apostles were brothers, friends, or close relatives of Jesus. It was their exclusive privilege to be His constant companion, and to receive His personal teachings.

Jesus prepared the Twelve for their future positions as the first Bishops of the Church. The dozen men served as witnesses to Jesus' Resurrection, and were charged with the responsibility for; establishing, guiding, directing, and the development of Christianity.

Since few people know the names of the Apostles, the following chart of the Twelve, and their relationship to each other is provided.

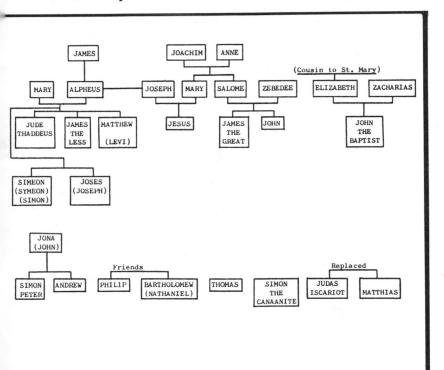

The Pharisees, leading progressive Judaic sect, believed their religion had to be interpreted, and updated to remain strong.

They made strict laws which controlled just about every human act. Each new rule became part of the Oral Law, considered as binding as the written law of the Bible. The Sadducees bitterly disagreed with the Pharisees, accepting only the written law. They refused to recognize the Oral Law as binding upon them.

The Pharisees, and Sadducees had been bitter political rivals, however both considered His philosophy revolutionary. They put their differences aside, and joined forces against the Intruder.

Everywhere Jesus spoke, large crowds of Jews, and Gentiles gathered *(non-Jews, heathens, pagans, foreigners, sinners)*. Religious leaders warned Jesus to avoid the Gentiles because under the Law *(Torah - the First Five Books of Moses)* it was strictly forbidden to preach the *Word of God* to anyone other than the Jews.

When Jesus ignored their threats, it was decided He had to be stopped before His revolutionary ideas caused a total disregard for their religious authority.

In the meantime, after months of instructions, and exposure to the demands of missionary life, the Apostles were sent out to teach Jesus' philosophy by word of mouth *(catechetical)*.

For their protection they were instructed to travel in apostolic fashion, two by two, and to address only the Jews in the nearby countryside of Galilee. *(Mk 6: 7-13, and Mk 10:5-9).*

As they passed through the villages preaching Jesus' message of love, they used the powers given to them to cure the sick from a variety of illnesses, and physical weaknesses. (Mt 10:1).

When they returned to Capernaum, Jesus wanted to know all about their experiences. He quickly realized the mission was far too great for just twelve men. As a solution He appointed 72 disciples as missionaries. *Jude's father was among them.*

> *Most of the names of the 72 missionaries have been lost to history. A few of the more famous names which survived are: Philip the Evangelist, and his prophetess daughters; Barnabas, (formerly Joseph); Matthias, who later replaced Judas Iscariot; Lazarus, whom Jesus brought back to life; and two men who became Jude's personal disciples during his missionary ministry, Mari and Abdias.*

As the final weeks of Jesus' earthly life was drawing near, the opening episode of a fascinating, two part story began which would concern Jude's later ministry.

The incident involved a *Prince Abgar V, of Edessa, Osroene,* and is popular in the Eastern Churches. *(Accounts of the legend have been recorded in various historical documents which are listed in the Bibliography and Commentary).*

> *Prince Abgar V, also known as: the Black; Abgarus; Ouchama; and King Abgar. He was the ruler of Osrhoene, a kingdom in northwestern Mesopotamia between the Tigris and Euphrates rivers (crossing the frontier of*

Turkey and Syria). Its capital was Edessa (now Urfa, Turkey).

According to historian *Eusebius,* Prince Abgar was suffering from a fatal disease, perhaps leprosy, when he heard about a holy man who was miraculously healing the sick.

Impressed by the reports, he dictated a letter to his secretary, Hannan, inviting Jesus to visit him in Edessa.   He gave the message to his courier with instructions to quickly find *the good Physician,* and deliver the invitation.   The courier located Jesus in Ephraim, and personally handed Him the message.

Some versions of the story say the messenger who carried the letter to Jesus was Abgar's trusted courier Ananias;   another, his secretary Hannan; a third, the Captain of the Guard, Cumra.

The following modern translation is said to be part of Prince Abgar's letter:

"Abgar, ruler of Osroene, to Jesus the excellent Savior who has appeared in the country of Jerusalem, greeting.   I have heard reports of You and of the cures You performed without medicine or herbs. I've concluded that one or two facts must be true; either, You are God, and having come down from heaven You do these things, or else, You who do these things is the Son of God.

"I have therefore written to ask if You would take the trouble to come to me and heal the disease which I have.   "I have heard that certain religious leaders are murmuring

*against You and plotting to injure You. I have
a very small, yet noble kingdom which is big
enough for us both."*

After reading the letter, Jesus explained to the
courier that He appreciated the Prince's invitation,
but regretfully had to decline. According to Eusebius, Jesus personally wrote out the following note to
the Prince:

*"Happy are you who have believed in Me
without having seen Me...In regard to what
you have written, that I should come to you, it
is necessary for Me to fulfill all things here for
which I have been sent and after I have finished My mission, I will be taken up again to
My Father who sent Me into the world.*
*"After I have ascended to Him, I'll send to
you one of My disciples, who shall heal your
sickness, and bring you and yours eternal
life."*

The Prince was encouraged by the reply, but
wanted to know what Jesus looked like. He directed
a court artist to go to Him, and draw His picture.
The artist located Jesus in the home of the *Chief of
the Jews, Gamaliel,* but, he was unable to fulfill his
assignment. When he tried to sketch Jesus his hand
would not respond.

Seeing the man's frustration, Jesus pressed a
square piece of white linen cloth to His face, and in
an instant His features were indelibly imprinted on
the material.

History is hazy as to whether the imprint-ed material was given to the artist for delivery to Abgar, or placed in Jude's care.

According to the Syriac document discov-ered by Church historian Eusebius, the fea-tures of Jesus on the linen cloth had "not-been-made-by-human-hands."

In Christian iconography, *The Holy Face of Edessa* is famous. For many years the mysterious portrait was kept with great reverence in Edessa.

Copies of the letters believed written by Jesus, and Abgar, along with reproductions of Jesus fea-tures, were good luck symbols.

Wording of both messages have been found en-graved on sills over doors in the ancient Greek city of Ephesus, *32* miles southeast of what is now *Izmir, Turkey.*

Copies were used by Anglo-Saxons as personal charms against; *"lightning, hail, perils by sea and land, by day and night, and in dark places."* Repro-ductions were encased in containers tied around men's arms.

In order to follow Jude's missionary ministry in sequence, it's necessary to interrupt the story at this point. The fascinating meeting of Jude, and Prince Abgar resumes in the upcoming chapter.

The final seven days of Jesus' earthly life was at hand *(Holy Week).* As the Apostles, and disciples walked with Him on the road to Jerusalem, they were worried for their safety.

Aware Jesus had enemies among the Pharisee, and Sadducee religious leaders, they realized it was not wise to go into the capital. They tried to persuade Him to turn back before it was too late, but Jesus was set on the distant city.

It was the Sunday before Passover as they approached Jerusalem *(Palm Sunday)*. Word of Jesus' arrival preceded Him, and the streets were overflowing with cheering followers.

As He passed through the city gates, His supporters formed a procession. It was customary to demonstrate affection for returning heroes by spreading clothing, and palm branches along the path. Jude and the others cautiously kept a safe distance to the rear.

Throughout the week Jesus told all who'd listen, that the Pharisees had added too many rules to the Law *(Torah)*. He warned the Jews to beware of their teachings, and made many disrespectful statements. The speech that caused the Apostles, and disciples the greatest worry was:

> *"...Woe upon you, scribes and Pharisees, you hypocrites that swallow up the property of widows, under cover of your prayers..."*
> *"...Serpents that you are, brood of vipers, how should you escape from the award of hell?..."*
> *(Matt 23:33 and Lk 11:37).*

A mortal clash between Jesus, the Pharisees, and Sadducees was inevitable. Religious leaders gathered in the Sanhedrin where they plotted to seize the Intruder, and have Him put to death. Judas Iscariot, the Apostle's treasurer, made a deal with the religious leaders to betray Him.

The Sanhedrin (Sanhedrim) was a 71 member governing council of Pharisee religious

leaders, and experts on Judaic Laws. It was
presided over by the Pharisee high priest.

A few hours before the dramatic events of the
Crucifixion were to unfold, Jesus, and the Apostles
shared the Passover meal together in the Upper
Room *(Last Supper)*. There, He promised those
gathered around the table, that after His death He
would return to them. He said:

"...Yet a little while and the world will no
longer see Me. But you will see Me, for I live
and you shall live..."

Jude couldn't understand why Jesus would not
present Himself to everyone, including the Gentiles.
The following is the only Gospel record of a conversation between Jude, and Jesus:

"..Lord, how is it that You will reveal
Yourself to us and not to the world?..."

Jesus indirectly responded to Jude's question as
He continued speaking:

"...If anyone loves Me, he will keep My
word, and My Father will love him, and We
will come to him and make Our home within
him...Peace I leave with you; My peace I give
to you..."* (Jn 14:19-22).

To retell the events leading to Jesus' crucifixion is
unnecessary for they should be familiar to all. However, to understand the closeness of Jude's family to
Jesus, several incidents must be reviewed:

As Jesus was being nailed to the cross, a huge crowd of curious spectators who had been following the public execution watched silently from a distance. Roman law clearly specified that only family members, and close personal friends of a condemned person were allowed to wait the long, agonizing deathwatch at the base of a cross. Those granted permission were:

> *Mary, Jesus' Mother; Mary of Cleophas, and the mother of Jude Thaddeus, James the Less, Joseph (Joses) and Matthew (Levi); Salome, the mother of John and James the Great; Mary Magdalen; and the Apostle John. (Jn 19:25-26).*

Overtaken with terror, ten of the Apostles, including Jude, and nearly all of the disciples went into hiding. Tradition records how Jude's brother, James the Less was so frightened, he hid all night in a vacant tomb in the cemetery.

Later, the Apostles, and disciples regrouped in the *Upper Room,* where only a few hours earlier they had shared the Last Supper with Jesus. Fearing the Pharisees, and Sadducees would be coming for them, they barred the doors.

Jesus' followers had no cause for concern, because the religious leaders had a more urgent problem. It was approaching sundown on Friday evening which marked the beginning of the *Sabbath.* Under *Mosaic Law,* it was a very serious sin for the bodies of the executed to be left hanging on the gibbet during the Sabbath.

Jesus, and the two thieves had to be removed from their crosses, and their bodies thrown into the criminal pit, or buried before nightfall. *(Deut. 21.23 and Jn 19:31)*.

The high priest in charge of the religious Sanhedrin went to Pontius Pilate, the Roman Governor of Judea, and asked him to order his soldiers to break the legs of three being crucified. *(crurifragium)*. *(Jn 19:32)*.

> *Breaking the leg bones of the condemned was accepted practice to hasten death. Without being able to support body weight, victims slumped, and quickly suffocated from the inability to draw air into their lungs.*

As requested, Pilate dispatched a military detail to attend to the matter. But, when the soldiers arrived at *Golgotha*, Jesus had already died. Since *Mosaic Law* also declared it a serious sin to break the bones of the dead, to be certain Jesus was not alive, a soldier stabbed Him in the side with his spear.

Joseph of Arimathea asked Pilate's permission to bury Jesus' body. With the help of Nicodemus, Jesus was wrapped in a linen cloth, and temporarily sealed in a nearby vault *(sepulcher)*.

The women who had stood by the cross went to their living quarters to prepare spices, and ointments to anoint Jesus' body for final interment on Sunday morning *(Easter Sunday)*.

Before dawn, *Jude's mother,* Mary Magdalen, Salome, Joanna, and another woman were ready. But, *Golgotha* was a dangerous place, so they had to wait until daybreak.

At the first blush of dawn, the women hurried along the road. When they arrived at the tomb, the huge stone which had sealed the entrance had been rolled back. Upon entering they discovered Jesus' body was gone *(Resurrection)*. In it's place was the burial cloth, *(Shroud of Turin)*.

The Shroud measures, (14' 3" x 3' 7) and is believed to bear the miraculous 2,000 year-old, three-dimensional image of Jesus. The blood stained material was kept as a relic until lost in the early 1200's. In 1355, it resurfaced in Lirey, France.

During the 1400's, the material was boiled in oil, and in water, but the stains remained. In 1532, it survived a fire; although singed around the edges.

Little was known about the Holy Shroud until 1578 when it was credited with the miraculous end to the deadly bubonic plague epidemic of Milan, Italy. "the plague lost all power over the people, and not another person died".

A chapel was constructed for the burial cloth in Turin, Italy where every May 4th, the Feast of the Holy Shroud, it was put on public view. In 1898, the Shroud was photographed, and when the film was developed, the negative showed that the cloth was a reversed negative in which black showed as white, and white as black. For the first time, the features of a face, and the outline of a man's full body could be seen imprinted in the material.

In 1978, forty American scientists were commissioned to examine the artifact. The material was subject to thousands of tests, involving more than 100,000 man hours.

After analysis of the findings, Kenneth Stevenson, the commission's spokesman stated that many pieces of evidence were in

> *keeping with the story of Jesus' Crucifixion.*
> *Gary Habermas, project consultant said; "it's*
> *possibly the holiest relic in Christendom"*
> *In 1983, Humbert II, the last exiled king of*
> *Italy turned ownership of the Shroud of Turin*
> *over to Pope John Paul II.*

Trembling with excitement, the women ran to give the Apostles, and disciples the news. On the way, *Jude's mother,* and the other women became the first to see Jesus. *(Matt 28:9).*

That afternoon, Jude's father *Alpheus,* and another disciple, were walking on the road leading to the village of Emmaus, when suddenly Jesus approached, and walked along with them. Later *Alpheus* rushed to Jerusalem to tell the disciples what had happened. *(Lk 24:13-36).*

When he found the group in the *Upper Room,* all were weeping in mourning. Jude's father told them to rejoice for Jesus was alive. While describing what had happened, Jesus appeared.

Believing He was a ghost, the Apostles, and most of the disciples huddled together in terror. Jesus tried to reassure them by saying; *"Peace be upon you, do not be afraid."*

Forty days later, at Bethany on Mount Olivet, *(Ascension Thursday),* Jesus told the Apostles, and disciples they were the foundation of His Church, and were to teach all nations.

After watching Him ascend, the realization of being alone again brought on an immediate loss of courage. Back in Jerusalem, about *120* disciples re-assembled in the *Upper Room,* and as before, locked themselves inside.

For nine consecutive days, *(the first novena)* all those in the *Upper* Room joined together in community prayer. On the morning of the ninth day, *(Pentecost Sunday)*, there came a sound like a roaring tornado, followed by what appeared to be tongues of fire which parted, and came to rest on each.

The noise was so loud a large number of foreign visitors in Jerusalem gathered outside the building. Jude and the others were bewildered when they joined the spectators, for they could understand every word being spoken even though the languages were foreign. *(Act 2: 1-12).*

For the remainder of their lives Jude and the others were no longer afraid. Through the powerful inspiration of the *Holy Spirit,* each received true courage, great strength of character, and unyielding faith.

CHAPTER VII

MISSIONARY ADVENTURES

With renewed enthusiasm, the Apostles, and disciples set about establishing a working organization to give the Church an operating form.

Historians *Epiphanius,* and *Eusebius,* recorded how the religious movement grew rapidly in Jerusalem, as large numbers of Jews were converted to the sect of Judaism called, the *New Israel, and Judeo-Christianity.*

From the beginning, the new sect of the Hebraic faith was a missionary movement. Several historians wrote that since Jude was the most experienced of the evangelists, he was the first sent out on a missionary assignment.

As he made his initial journey south to the ancient kingdom of Idumea, *(Edom, Siere, Mount Seir),* in all probability he was accompanied by his wife, children, and a companion disciple.

For years the small group walked from one community to another as Jude preached Jesus' words. Legend says the Apostle Thomas, who was charged with assigning missionaries, was divinely inspired to send Jude to *Edessa.*

The story which began in the previous chapter, concerning the exchange of letters between Jesus, and Prince Abgar, resumes at this point in Jude's missionary adventures.

According to historian *Eusebius*, Jude along with his disciple Mari, *(one of the original 72 disciples)*, traveled overland *400* miles northeast to the inland city of *Edessa*.

Upon arrival, they were welcomed into the Jewish home of *Tobias, the son of Tobias,* where they remained as his guests.   In keeping with custom, Jude first addressed a small colony of Edessene Jews, before preaching to the Gentiles.

Wherever he spoke, large crowds gathered.   The people were fascinated by his extraordinary power to call on the Lord to miraculously cure the physically handicapped.

When the Prince was told about the holy man who was in the city performing wonders, he knew it had to be the *promised one*.   A messenger was quickly dispatched to invite the *wonder worker* to the palace.

When brought before him, Jude placed his hands on the Prince, and *by the word of Jesus,* Abgar was instantly healed of his disease.   In the same moment, all others of the Prince's court who'd been suffering illnesses, were also cured.

Abgar tried to reward Jude with precious gems, gold, and land, but the missionary only asked permission to move freely throughout the kingdom. With the Prince's blessing, Jude and Mari traveled the territory preaching the good news.

Legend records how they evangelized the city of Nisibin *(Nisibis, now called Nusaybin, Turkey)*.   It was there Mari became ill, and died.

For an unspecified period, Jude worked alone. Before he moved on to the independent province of the *kingdom of Armenia,* Jude Thaddeus had converted many wandering Arabs to Christianity.   Included among the number were: the Prince, his family, and court; the Royal Jeweler, *Aggai* who became the Bishop of Edessa; and *Palut,* a citizen Jude ordained a priest.

Armenia was unlike the smaller territory of Osroene. Converting the people of the mountainous country in western Asia, was a huge undertaking. On occasion, Jude was assisted by the Apostles; Andrew, Simon the Zealot, Bartholomew *(Nathaniel),* Matthias, and many disciples.

Regardless of the number of missionaries who labored in the kingdom on the Black Sea, Armenian national legends, and traditions are rich with stories about how Jude converted thousands. In fact, Armenian Christians insist it was Jude who was the founder of their religion.

> *Bishop Melchizedec Mouriandantz of the Armenian National Church stated in the 19th century, that his people believe there is no difference between Peter, and Jude.*

According to ancient writings, when Jude left Armenia, he traveled far to the north. Some documents say he preached in Tbilisi, or Tiflis, *(a city about 150 miles north of Mount Ararat, Turkey, near the borders of Russia, and Iran).*

From there he made his way *340* miles to the southeast, to Baku, *(today a key Russian city on the Caspian Sea).* Some historians claim there is substantial evidence supporting the conclusion that Jude's ministry went all the way to the Roman province of Tripolitania, and Cyrenaica, *(now Libya), on the northern coast of Africa.*

Regardless of the exact boundaries of his missionary journeys, for nearly *35* years Jude was away in distant lands. By the time he reported to the Church Council on his activities, he was 65 years old. During the *three-and-a-half decades* he was away, Judeo-Christianity had undergone many dramatic changes:

> *Twenty-three years earlier (A.D. 42) the "Council of Jerusalem" had been formed as the final deciding body on all matters affecting the growth, and development of the Church.*
>
> *Jude's brother, James the Less had been appointed first Bishop of the Church of Jerusalem. However, two decades later (A.D. 62) he was martyred. Eusebius wrote in his History of the Christian Church (Hist. Eccl. ii. 23: 1-19), that the religious Sanhedrin, for political reasons, or out of envy, ordered his stoning.*
>
> *St. Epiphanius recorded how James' older brother Symeon, (Simeon - Simon), publicly spoke out against the disgraceful execution. It is believed that since he assisted James in governing the Church, he was appointed the second Bishop of Jerusalem.*
>
> *As for Jude's other brothers, Matthew carried on as a missionary in several nations; suffering a martyrs death.*
>
> *Nothing is recorded about the activities of Joses (Joseph), however, a few historians suggest he also served as an active missionary disciple.*
>
> *Alpheus, Jude's father, suffered martyrdom for his outspoken devotion to Jesus. Any reliable information about the fate of Jude's mother is lacking.*
>
> *With the missionary expansion of Christianity throughout the ancient world, the*

number of Gentile converts grew increasingly large. By the A.D. 60's, they were in the majority, and the religion began revolving almost entirely around the person, and teachings of Jesus.

Instead of conforming to the Judaic rites, ceremonies, customs, and rules Gentile converts began thinking of themselves as belonging to an independent religion, and the movement slowly drifted away from the parent Hebraic faith.

In A.D. 65, while Jude was awaiting a missionary assignment, the high priest of Palestinian Judaism ordered the Judeo-Christian converts, both Jew and Gentile to conform to all of the religious doctrines, and customs of Mosaic Law.

When the Church Council refused, the religion of Jesus was no longer accepted as a part of Judaism, and those of the new faith were called, "Christians."

Meanwhile, according to the *Apostolic History of Abdias,* and the *Ten Books of Craton,* Jude was teamed up with Simon the Zealot. The two elderly Apostles, accompanied by their personal disciples, Craton and Abdias, left Antioch on a long overland journey to Persia *(now Iran)* in the heart of the Parthian Empire.

When they arrived in Babylon *(now Al Hillah, Iraq)* the Parthian government was in the midst of violent change. For years conditions of state had been deteriorating under the poor reign of King Vologaeses I *(Volagases I - A.D. r.51-79).*

Since the mid-lst century, B.C. bitter rivalry had raged between Parthia, and Rome resulting in several major military conflicts. Vologaeses held a deep hatred for everything Roman, and was suspicious of all foreigners, including the alien religion of Christianity.

According to *Abdias' history,* a significant incident happened to Jude and Simon shortly after their arrival in Babylon. General Varadach (*Baradac - Varadac),* the commander-in-chief of the king's army was preparing to engage a strong invading enemy force.

Whenever important issues of state were at risk, it was customary to summon *Babylonian Magi* to obtain a prophesy from the pagan gods. Such was the situation when *Zaroes and Arfaxat* were ordered to ask the pagan gods to foretell the outcome of the impending battle.

The magicians were involved in a life threatening predicament. If they told the general the gods forecast victory, and the battle was lost; or if defeat was foretold, and the outcome was victory; they would be branded imposters. The penalty for such a crime was public execution.

Pain of stones on their bodies was fresh in their memories, for not many years before they had been run out of Abyssinia when *Jude's brother Matthew* exposed them as impostors.

To avoid giving a prophesy, *the Magi* told the general the gods refused to speak because magicians of a foreign western God were in the city.

The general ordered the Apostles brought before him. After a lengthy interrogation, he told the two Apostles he knew about their power to silence the gods. He ordered them to predict the outcome of the pending military campaign.

Instead of a direct response, Jude asked the general to command *the Magi* to make another try at communicating with the idols. The request was granted leaving *Zaroes and Arfaxat* no alternative but to come up with a prediction.

Believing the invading enemy force had the strength to carry on a long military campaign, they told the general the idols had finally spoken, but the news was not good. The gods had revealed the battle would develop into a long, and hard fought war with great suffering, and death to both sides.

Upon hearing the prediction, Jude spoke up saying *the Magi's gods* had lied, because at daybreak messengers from the invading force would come forward with a peace pact. Not knowing who to believe, the general ordered the Apostles, and *Magi* placed under close guard.

At dawn, as Jude had predicted, ambassadors arrived from the enemy camp with an attractive peace offer. The missionaries were immediately released, and *the Magi* ordered put to death.

Jude and Simon pleaded with the general to spare *the magicians'* lives. Impressed by their show of compassion, he granted the request. However, instead of gratitude, *Zaroes and Arfaxat* hated the missionaries, and became a constant source of distress.

The Magi plagued the aging Apostles with persistent slanderous campaigns. They used their skills as magicians to trick people into believing their pagan idols were more powerful than the Christian God. But, Jude and Simon always managed to outwit the cunning pair.

Legendary records indicated that before Jude and Simon left the Parthian Empire, they had converted some *60,000* people to Christianity. To care for the spiritual needs of the new flock, they used their authority as bishops to consecrate *Abdias,* first Bishop of Babylon.

The Roman author Fabricius, who quoted an earlier source, wrote that Jude and Simon labored as missionaries for about *14* years. Some historians suggest that from time to time they returned to Edessa, Armenia, and other cities for periods of rest. Some scholars suggest it was during one of these interludes when Jesus' cousin composed the *"Epistle of Jude." (App C).*

In *A.D. 79,* Jude and Simon entered the city of Susa *(Suanir or Samir - Latin, Suanis civitate Persarum).* As they approached the square they saw what looked to be nearly the entire population, including the *70* priests of the local pagan temples.

Zaroes and Arfaxat had arrived several days earlier, and had stirred the people to the brink of violence. The Apostles tried to tell the excited mob that the sun, moon, and animals whom the people were worshiping as gods, were nothing more than the creations of the one true God.

The mob refused to listen, and the Apostles were ordered to kneel in worship before the heathen idols, or face death. In response, the missionaries ordered the demon spirits inside the pagan idols to depart.

Instantly, the statues toppled from their pedestals; shattering to the ground. Two hideous figures appeared in the rubble, and fled the temple in rage; howling in blasphemy. Even after witnessing the exorcism, *(the religious driving away of evil spirits),* Jude and Simon were attacked by the mob.

The manner in which they were martyred is not known with absolute certainty. According to legend, however, they were beaten with clubs, or large sticks, and pelted with stones.

Jude was clubbed unconscious, run through with a spear, and decapitated with a broadaxe *(an ancient military weapon).* Simon was sawed, or chopped into pieces.

As their lives were drawing to a bloody end; perhaps in their final moments they recalled Jesus' words:

> "...*all the world will be hating you because you bear My name; but the person will be saved, who endures to the last...*" *(Mk 13:13).*

....

A *2nd century* list of burial places of the Apostles, includes Jude Thaddaeus in the square *(caste)* in Edessa. Another translation says he was entombed in a castle *(beritha)* along the Osroenian coast.

A different legend says that on the third anniversary of Jude's martyrdom, *King Xerxes* had his body entombed within a new octagonal temple in Babylon.

Still, another account claims he was taken to Edessa by faithful friends where he was given temporary burial in a secret grave.

Regardless of his resting place, without an obituary, *Jude Thaddeus, Apostle became a forgotten saint.*

SYMBOLS IDENTIFIED WITH ST. JUDE

Since the *A.D. 400's,* few likenesses of Jesus, and the saints have been created in Christian art without a ring, or an area of radiance above the head (halo, also known as nimbus, aureole, or glory).

In Roman Catholicism, a number of saints are shown with emblems by which they can be easily identified. Martyrs are customarily represented in statuary, and art along with the instruments of torture used to take their lives.

St. Jude Thaddeus is often shown holding a knotted club, or large sticks for the types of weapons believed used to take his life. Sometimes he is associated with a broadaxe, or halberd (miltiary axe) to symbolize his decapitation.

A flame is frequently displayed above his head, representing the Holy Spirit descending upon him as tongues of fire. The flame is also for the gift of tongues which he received at Pentecost.

Jesus' cousin is generally holding a medallion, or portrait of Jesus' features, which represents "The Holy Face of Edessa."

Less often he is shown holding a book which is representative of the "Epistle of St. Jude."

In East Anglican art, he's with a ship, or an anchor. The Shrine of St. Jude in San Francisco emphasizes the anchor as a symbol of hope.

San Francisco

New York City

New Orleans

Chicago, Dominican

City of St. Jude

New York City

Chicago, Ntl Shrine

Baltimaore Shrine

Quebec, Ntl Shrine

CHAPTER VIII

SAINT OF SAINTS

Sixteen years after Jude's martyrdom, toward the end of the reign of Roman Emperor Domitian, (r. 81-97), two of Jude's grandsons, *Zoker and James* became part of his historical portrait.

Accounts of the incident were recorded by the Jewish-Christian historian *Hegesippus,* and later translated by Church historian *Eusebius.*

The story began when *Emperor Domitian,* a ruthless tyrant who behaved like a madman, heard a prophecy about a descendant of *the House of King David* who would overthrow kingdoms, and powers.

Concerned about the threat of a rebellion, he ordered all descendants of the royal line of Israel be rounded up. A manhunt produced *Zoker and James,* cousins of the promised Messiah.

They were brought before *Domitian,* and for several days interrogated about their ancestry, and the kingdom of Jesus. The young men maintained their innocence; insisting they knew nothing of a plot to overthrow the emperor.

Zoker and James tried to make *Domitian* understand Jesus' kingdom was not of this world, but a spiritual kingdom. Only after being satisfied there was nothing to fear from the peasant farmers, did the emperor set them free. (*Nothing more is known about Jude's grandsons*).

For six centuries Jude Thaddeus was forgotten to most of the world, and his remains left undisturbed. Then, in the *mid-600's* a new enemy of Christianity,

Arabs *(Mohammedans-Moslems)* of the Islamic religion, defeated the Persians.

> *To avoid desecration of St. Jude's burial site, Armenian Catholic leaders who kept their patron saints memory alive, exhumed his skeletal remains, and transported them to Rome. However, his forearm bone was kept in Armenia as a national relic.*

The next notable incident involving another relic of St. Jude began in *A.D. 799*, when *Pope Leo III* was driven from Rome by his enemies.

A distress message was sent by the pope to the most powerful monarch in Europe, *Frankish King Charlemagne.* The king was a dedicated protector of the Roman Church, and in response marched his military forces to Rome. In a short time he put down the revolt, and restored Leo to his throne.

> *On Christmas Day, A.D. 800, in the Cathedral of Saint Peter, Pope Leo III expressed his appreciation by crowning Charlemagne,* Emperor of the Western Roman Empire.
>
> *He also gave him several saints' relics, including St. Jude's. Charlemagne carried the holy treasures back to France where they were enshrined in Toulouse, in the Cathedral of St. Saturninus.*
>
> *In the course of centuries, devotion to the relics gradually decreased, and they were eventually misplaced.*

In the *1050's*, Armenia had been overrun by the champions of Islam, *the Seljuk Turks.* The Armenian Catholics who had been protecting Jude's relic forearm were worried for its safety, so they fled to Turkey. There the relic was preserved in the Holy Rosary Church in Izmire, on the eastern coast of the Aegean Sea.

The Dominicans' involvement with St. Jude's forearm bone began in the mid 1200's when Armenian Catholic leaders faced the reality they could no longer guarantee the relic's safety. To be sure it didn't fall into heathen hands, it was sent to the Dominican's in Turin, Italy.

Periodically throughout the centuries, prominent devotees have focused attention on St. Jude's life, and works:

In the early to mid-11th century, (St). Bernard of Clairvaux (1090-1153), whose motto was "Love Serves", was noted for a strong devotion to St. Jude. He was never without a relic of his patron saint; "his special protector".

His dying request was to have the relic placed over his heart, and buried with him so even in death he would not be separated from his patron saint.

During the mid-1300's, a Swedish nun, (St.) Bridget, (Birgitta-Brigitta 1302-1373), was noted for her charitable, saintly life, and extraordinary apparitions.

In one vision, Jesus instructed her to turn to St. Jude in prayer with confidence because: "..he will show himself most willing to give help.." In another, Jesus directed her to dedicate: "...the fifth altar" to St. Jude in her church..."

In 1478, a priest whose name is lost to history, appealed to the authorities at the Cathedral of St. Saturninus in Toulouse to make an effort to locate his patron saint's missing relic.

His rigid determination resulted in a search which produced not only St. Jude's relic, but all the others as well. Not satisfied, he hounded authorities until St. Jude's relic was put on permanent display inside the Cathedral.

Before the end of the 15th century a Dominican Nun, (St.) Columba of Rieti (1467-1501), dedicated a large part of her religious calling to St. Jude.

She told all who would listen, how she had been privileged to bear witness to the answering of prayers of "grave, and serious nature" through her patron saint's intercessory power.

On *October 31, 1517,* an incident took place which had a lasting impact on Christianity, and in a roundabout way also involved St. Jude's relic remains in Rome.

Martin Luther, a Roman Catholic monk, and professor of theology was vehemently against the selling of *Plenary Indulgences* by Pope Leo X, and nailed the famous *"Ninety-Five Theses"* on the door of the Castle Church.

Plenary Indulgence *is full pardon from all temporary (temporal) punishment which re-*

mains owed after receiving forgiveness (absolution) of sins through confession, (sacrament of Penance - Reconciliation).

Partial Indulgence *is the pardon of some of the temporary punishment which remains owed after sins have been forgiven through* sacramental absolution.

Luther's public outcry stirred so much negative controversy, *indulgences* were just about completely eliminated by Popes; Leo X, Adrian VI, Clement VII, and Paul III. Therefore, it was an act of major significance when:

On September 22, 1548, Pope Paul III, (r. 1534-1550), granted a Plenary *Indulgence to all who visited St. Jude's tomb in Rome on the saint's feast day.*

In 1620, Pope Paul V (r. 1605-1621) directed attention to St. Jude by ordering an altar built in St. Peter's Basilica in honor of the forgotten saint.

On December 27, 1605, with ceremony, St. Jude's relic remains were permanently set under the center altar; the very spot where St. Peter had been crucified. All present received a Plenary *Indulgence.*

For *200* years no significant devotion to St. Jude can be found. Then, in the *mid-1800's,* several un-related events happened which indirectly led to his rediscovery.

The Dominican Fathers, and other Roman Catholic missionary orders were very active in Europe.

In Spain, a Jesuit, Father (St.) Antony Claret (1807-1870), was busy establishing "the congregation of Missionary Sons of the Immaculate Heart of Mary," (Claretians).

It was during this era that a book was published in Italy and Spain about the life, and works of St. Jude.

Through the publication, details about the the life and works of the forgotten Apostle found its way to the missionaries of the various orders.

It took nearly a half century *(1911)* before the first breakthrough occurred. The Claretian missionaries working in Chile built a shrine in St. Jude's honor.

No sooner had the final stone been put in place, than people began visiting the shrine to ask St. Jude for his intercessory help.

Word about the saint who came to the aid of people in desperation radiated to other South American countries.

How devotion to St. Jude came to the United States is a fascinating story. It began in Prescott, Arizona, a small mining, agricultural, and resort region about *135* miles northwest of Phoenix. The person who served as the instrument was *Father James Tort,* a Claretian assigned to the local mission church.

In *1923,* the missionary priest happened across a *St. Jude prayer card.* He found the prayer interesting, and began reciting it as a regular part of his daily spiritual exercise.

Several months later, *Father Tort* was suddenly transferred to Chicago's southeast side to take charge of construction of *Our Lady of Guadalupe Church.*

For the next four years the project limped along; always short of funds. In *1927*, even though the interior was unfinished, the small church opened to the public for worship services.

A few weeks later, an immigrant parishioner donated a statue of St. Jude to the new church. Surprised by the gift, *Father Tort* placed it next to that of St. Therese of Lisieux *(the Little Flower of Jesus).*

Father Tort had hoped financial conditions would improve after the church opened. Yet, the scarcity of money remained critical because most of the congregation were the families of poorly paid laborers who worked in nearby steel mills.

The future of the neighborhood parish looked dark, and *Father Tort* feared the project would have to be abandoned.

With the *1928* Lenten season approaching, the missionary announced that although not customary, *two novenas* would be held during the same nine days. One, in honor of St. Therese for vocations, the other to St. Jude for needed financial help.

St. Therese's statue was moved to the front of the sanctuary, while St. Jude's remained in its place. But, to Father Tort's surprise most of the parishioners favored the St. Jude novena.

So many people were praying before St. Jude's statue, that he decided to move it to a more convenient position on the right side of the sanctuary; *where it remains today.*

In the autumn, a *Solemn St. Jude Novena* was held, but the number of devotees had become so great, that on the final night of the novena *(Oct 28th, St. Jude's feast day)* hundreds of people were disappointed for there was no room inside the unfinished church.

As the weeks passed, a steady stream of pilgrims from other parishes visited the modest chapel. Donations were not overflowing, but ample money was provided to complete the church, support the spiritual, and some of the social welfare needs of the parish.

With the approval of *Cardinal Mendelein* of Chicago, documentation of all that had transpired in the little church was sent to Rome.

Upon completion of an extensive investigation, on *February 17, 1929,* Pope Pius XI, gave his blessings to establish the *"National Shrine to St. Jude"* as the *"Mother" American shrine of devotion to the patron saint* within Chicago's, Our Lady of Guadalupe Church.

The pope also declared *Plenary Indulgences* for several feasts held in the shrine during each year, including a *Partial Indulgence* for every prayer recited in honor of St. Jude.

The largest first-class relic in North America, believed to be one of St. Jude's shinbones, was sent from Rome. It was placed in a container *(reliquary)* on the saint's altar, where it is presented for public veneration during novenas.

> *A saint's relic may be the mortal remains of a deceased holy person. It can be an entire preserved body, a lifelike member such as a hand, tongue, or a minute chip of bone. More loosely, a relic can be any object associated with a saint's life. Every Catholic Church has at least one saint's relic sealed within its consecrated altar, or altar stone.*

In the summer of *1929,* there was a noticeable increase in the number of local families attending novena services at the shrine. The sudden show of devotion was inspired out of fear of financial ruin, as the steel mills were cutting back on work forces.

Interest in St. Jude had now spread all over the windy city. Across town the *Dominican Fathers at St. Pius Church* in the heart of Chicago, were being petitioned by parishioners to start St. Jude novena services.

Consequently, on *October 20, 1929,* the first *Solemn St. Jude Novena* was held by the Dominican Fathers. The response was amazing and in a short time plans were underway to establish a second official *St. Jude Shrine* in Chicago.

Meanwhile, a disastrous drama was unfolding. For years financial experts had been predicting an economic collapse of major proportions. Fear of doom was being whispered as worker pressure mounted with the loss of more and more jobs.

The day after St. Jude's feast day, *(October 29, 1929),* the expected finally happened; the stock market crashed. Businesses and banks failed, factories and steel mills shut down, stores closed; industry was paralyzed.

Within a matter of weeks, millions of people lost every penny of their savings. By the new year, *90* percent of Chicago's labor force were without paychecks. To feed hungry families, unemployed workers waited in long bread lines for free food.

As in every major disaster, churches of all denominations were filled to capacity. Men, women, and children were attending St. Jude novena services at both Chicago churches.

When people saw prayers being answered, word about the intercessory power of St. Jude spread from one end of the nation to the other.

Pope Pius XII gave his blessings to the *Shrine of Saint Jude Thaddeus* within Chicago's St. Pius Church.

The relic of St. Jude's forearm bone which had been given to *the Dominican Order in Turin, Italy in the mid-1200's* by the Armenian Catholics, was presented to the new shrine.

> *Dominican Superior, the Very Reverend Raphael Tavano, said he was inspired to give St. Jude's relic to his Dominican brethren at the Chicago shrine because: "...the relic belongs where devotion to St. Jude flourishes..."*
>
> *Today, the treasured forearm of St. Jude is an object of great religious devotion. It is exposed on the altar on the last day of each of five yearly novenas.*
>
> *The holy relic is contained in a silver casting of a life-size forearm. The hand is partially opened with the forefinger, and thumb extended as in Benediction.*
>
> *Within the silver form is a glass section through which the relic may be viewed. The metal of the case has been examined by qualified silversmiths who all agree on its ancient quality, and design.*

The St. Jude movement spread to *Our Lady of Guadalupe* Church in New Orleans. A committee of parishioners whose prayers had been answered through St. Jude, asked their pastor to hold a public novena in honor of their patron saint.

A St. Jude statue was placed in a side niche, and on Sunday, *January 6, 1935,* the Oblate Fathers held two St. Jude novena services.

Devotees came from all over and in a short time the New Orleans chapel was so crowded additional novenas had to be added. In time, plans were in motion to obtain papal permission for the *"International Shrine of St. Jude."*

While this was happening, on the other side of the nation in San Francisco, California, the Dominicans of the Province of the Holy Name were in the process of forming the *"Shrine of Saint Jude Thaddeus"* within St. Dominic's Church.

On the East Coast, the Franciscan Friars received permission from Pope Pius XII to create the *"Shrine of St. Jude"* within St. Stephen of Hungary church in New York City.

As St. Jude's popularity was rapidly growing, President Roosevelt was deeply involved in the mammoth job of trying to stabilize the economy.

At the same time, clouds of global armed conflict were gathering on the horizon. By the end of *1941,* America was involved in *WW II.*

Shortly after the outbreak of fighting, the Pallottine Fathers began novena services in honor of the "Patron in Cases Despaired of" for the parishioners of *St. John the Baptist Roman Catholic Church* in downtown Baltimore, Maryland.

Fear of injury, and death to loved ones fighting in far-off lands attracted worried relatives from beyond the city limits to the novena services.

Devotions to St. Jude grew so rapidly that additional novena services had to be added. Before long, St. John the Baptist Church was being called Baltimore's center of the "Patron Saint of Difficult Cases."

During the dozen years following the Depression, people had been praying through St. Jude to financially survive. Before they could get off their knees, they were praying for an end to the bloodiest, and costliest war the world had ever known.

In *August, 1945,* with the explosion of two atomic bombs over *Hiroshima, and Nagasaki* the war abruptly ended.

During the five years of fighting, the scars of the Depression had healed, and as the fighting men returned home everything went back as before.

With industry converting to peacetime production, the United States entered the greatest period of economic growth in the history of civilization.

With peace and prosperity interest in formal religion dropped off sharply. Before long there was an abundance of empty seats in the nation's churches, and synagogues.

Yet, devotions to St. Jude continued growing. Four years after the war, *1949,* at the request of masses of Canadian devotees, the *National Shrine of St. Jude* was inaugurated in Montreal, Quebec.

It's amazing that prior to the *1929 Depression,* St. Jude was a relatively obscure saint. Yet, two decades later he was being honored in nearly every nation of the world.

Father Joachim De Prada, late director of the National Shrine to St. Jude in Chicago, stated: "...*There are probably more churches in the United States being dedicated to St. Jude than to any other single saint, with the exception of St. Mary...*"

APPENDIX A

JUDE AND HIS FAMILY TREE

JUDE THADDEUS was one of the original Twelve Apostles. In the New Testament he is referred to in several ways.

> *Judas the brother of James (Acts 1:14).*
> *Jude the brother of James (Lk 6:16)*
> *Thaddaeus (Mt 10:3, and Mk 3:19).*
> *Judas (Mk 6:3 and Mt 13:55).*

Only after *Judas Iscariot's* name was dropped from the list of Apostles, and replaced by Matthias, was the name "*Jude*" first recorded.

To avoid confusion, early Christian writers were careful to use different names to distinguish *Judas Iscariot* from *Jude* (Judas) *Thaddeus* (Thaddaeus). John obviously didn't want any confusion, so he wrote, *"Judas, not the Iscariot"* (Jn 14:22).

In the ancient world of the Apostles, common people didn't have last names. For purposes of identification, personal characteristics, trades, places of birth, and various other titles were tagged onto given names.

During the time of Jesus' ministry, among the most common methods of identification was to add the name of a person's home town such as; *Jesus of Nazarath, Judas Iscariot (from Kerioth), etc.*

It was Greek custom for a man to be distinguished from others with the same name, by adding his father's name, for example: *Jude son of Alpheus.* If a relative, such as a brother, an uncle, or a cousin, was better known than the father, that person's name was sometimes added.

This was the case with Jude's brother, *James the Less,* who was prominent in the early Christian community. Undoubtedly, that's why Jude was sometimes referred to as: *Jude brother of James.*

The 1611 King James Version of the Bible identifies Jude as "Judas son of James". Later, the "Revised Standard and New English Versions" corrected the mistranslation to, "Judas the brother of James".

Because of the merging, and extinction of ancient languages the task of establishing the identity of a particular person of history is often difficult.

Some of the early writers compounded the problem by handling spelling carelessly. It's not unusual for one person to appear in the same document with different spellings.

To complicate matters even further, over the centuries many ancient words changed definition several times, or have become obsolete with no modern meaning.

Then, there is the obstacle of the translation of names from one language to another. History is filled with Hebrew, Greek, Latin, and Aramaic names.

Aramaic was the language of the Near East from 100 B.C. to A.D. 700. In fact, Jesus and the disciples spoke an Aramaic dialect, the popular language of Palestine.

Studying the various translated names of Jude Thaddeus provides an inkling of the difficulties involved in establishing absolute identities:

Judah, *(Judas or Jude)* was the most common of all Hebrew names for it had been the name of the founder of the tribe of Judah, one of the twelve tribes of Israel.

In Aramaic; Jude (Judah or Judas) is *"Yehuda"*. In Greek; it's *"Ioudas"*.

(St.) Luke identified Jude as; "Joudas Iakabou", or "adelphos de Iakabou"; meaning, *"Jude of James";* or Greek for *"Judas, the brother of James"*.

In the Apostolic Constitutions dealing with the administration, and structure of the early Church, and in some versions of Matthew, Jude is called *"Thaddaeus",* while in others *"Lebbaeus"*.

This is not as confusing as it appears for Thaddaeus *(Thaddeus),* and Lebbaeus *(Labbeus),* according to most philologists *(experts in the science of languages)* are merely different Greek versions of the: Hebrew *"Theudas",* or *"Libbai",* or *"Leb"* meaning, heart, hearty, or of the heart.

In Aramaic, Thaddeus is *"Taddai"* or *"tad"* which means, broad, barrel-chested, or large-breasted. *"Thaddeus"* could have been used to describe Jude's personality, for the word also translated into: beloved, generous, bighearted, courageous, or kind-hearted.

Perhaps *"Thaddaeus, or Lebbaeus"* was a descriptive nickname used much like today in describing a person's prominent physical features such as; Red, Rusty, Lefty, Slim, Tiny, Shorty, etc.

A few researchers believe that *"Thaddaeus"* was simply an early mistranslation error of *"Theudas"* which meant Judas.

Jude's name has long been popular in Ireland where in the old Gaelic it's *"Taidg"*.

Children everywhere are today named in honor of the Apostle; *Jude, Judith, Thaddeus, and Thad.*

Some scholars have concluded the primary reason St. Jude was lost to history was due to his numerous names, and titles.

Also in the "Biblical list of Apostles", the "Litany of the Saints", and until recently the "Canon of the Roman Catholic Mass", Jude is referred to only by his descriptive name *"Thaddeus"*.

Omission of his given name, along with the complication of two Apostles having the same first names, *(Judas Thaddaeus, and Judas Iscariot)*, has, and to some degree, still causes confusion.

Finally, there are the different beliefs of the Eastern Orthodox, and Western Roman Catholic churches.

The Eastern Rite accepts a Syriac tradition which says the founder of the Church of Edessa was not Jude Thaddeus, but rather one of the 72 disciples named *Addai*.

Philologists, however, point out that *Addai* is Syriac for *Thaddaeus*. Therefore, some scholars concede that *St. Addai,* was perhaps a missionary around Edessa toward the end of the 2nd century, (A.D. 180).

Then there is the legend that says *St. Addai* died in peace either in Edessa or the seaboard town of Beyrut, a port on the Osroenian coast.

It's interesting to note that the feast of St. Addai is celebrated with *St. Mari* on Aug 5.

As for *St. Jude Thaddaeus,* the Greek Orthodox Church celebrates the feast of *"St. Judas, Apostle, and Brother of the Lord"* on June 19, and *"St Thaddaeus Apostle"* on Aug 21.

The Roman Catholic Church's, "Romano-Gallican service books" *(8th century)* joined St. Jude's feast date with St. Simon the Zealot on Oct 28.

ALPHEUS (Alphaeus, Clopas, Cleopas, or Cleophas), according to the 2nd century Church historian *Hegesippus,* was *(St.)* Joseph's brother, and therefore Jesus' uncle. (His. eccl., III.11; IV.22).

Jude's father, *Alpheus,* was one of the most faith of Jesus' 72 disciples as evidenced by his name appearing seven times throughout the New Testament:

"..James the son of Alphaeus..." (Mt 10:4, Lk 6:15, and Mk 3:18).

"..And one of them, who was called Cleophas, answered Him..." (Lk 24:18).

"...Mary the wife of Cleophas (Clopas)..." (Jn 19:25).

"...James the son of Alphaeus...and Judas the brother of James..." (Acts 1:13).

"...Levi, the son of Alphaeus..." (Mk 2:14).

CLOPAS *(Cleopas or Alphaeus)* is believed by many scholars to be the Greek name for the Hebrew "Halphai"; Aramaic "Chalpai".

Alphaeus was a Greek name, yet, during the 1st century it was used by the Jewish inhabitants of Palestine.

St. Jerome, one of the most scholarly interpreters of the Bible, identified *Alphaeus with Cleophas.*

Some time after Pentecost, Cleophas *(Alphaeus)* was murdered because of his outspoken devotion to Jesus. His name is entered in the martyrology with a feast date of September 25.

MARY OF ALPHEUS (Cleophas) was a young Galilean girl, and Jude's mother.

Like today, "Mary, Maria, Mara, Mirya, Miriam, or Mariam" was a common name in Palestine during the 1st century.

Jude's mother was the sister-in-law of Jesus' Mother. However, a few researchers claim that the "Mary" referred to in the writings, wasn't Alpheus' wife, but rather his daughter.

This interpretation is very doubtful since Jewish women were never identified by the addition of their father's name.

Some other historians suggest that Joseph, and Alpheus were brothers who married sisters.

Likewise, this theory has little merit, because it was not customary for Jewish families to give daughters the same name.

Another group of scholars claim Jesus' maternal grandmother, *Anne,* and Jude's grandfather, *James* were brother, and sister.

Other historians suggest *Jesus' grandmother, Anne,* and *Jude's maternal grandmother* were sisters.

Nonetheless, Scripture calls attention to Jude's mother in several different ways:

"..Mary the mother of James and Joseph.."
(Mt 27:56).
"..Mary the mother of James.." (Lk 24:10, and
Mk 16:1)
"..Mary the mother of James the Less and of
Joseph.." (Mk 15:40).
"..Mary the wife of Cleophas (Clopas).." (Jn
19:25).
"..Mary the mother of Joseph.." (Mk 15:47).
"..and the other Mary with her.." (Mt 27:61)
"..and the other Mary came near.." (Mt 28:1)

Jude's mother is credited with having petitions granted through her heavenly intervention. Her feast date is April 9.

JUDE'S BROTHERS

Saints Ambrose, Hilary, and Gregory of Tour, among other theologians, agree that Alpheus' sons were first cousins to Jesus. The Gospels of Matthew, and Mark record:

"...Is not this the carpenter's Son, whose
Mother is called Mary, and His brethren,
James (the Less), Joseph (Joses), Simon
(Simeon or Symeon); and Judas (Jude Thad-
deus)?..." (Mt 13:55, and Mk 6:3).

Jude's brother Matthew *(Levi)* is not mentioned in the above chapters, however, he is referred to as; "...*Levi, the son of Alphaeus...*" (Mk 2:14).

MATTHEW (Levi), is believed to have been the only "Publican" (Latin Publicani - prosperous tax-collector) among the Apostles. (Mt 10:3).

According to St. John Chrysostom, this information is not altogether correct because *Matthew, and his brother James the Less* were employed as customs officers at the Palestinian lake port of Capernaum *(Capharnaum):*

"*..Jesus saw a man called Matthew sitting at work in the customs-house..*" *(Mt 9:9).*
"*..(Jesus) caught sight of a publican, called Levi, sitting at work in the customs house..*" *(Lk 5:27).* "*..(Jesus) saw Levi, the son of Al-phaeus, sitting at work in the customs-house..*" *(Mk 2:14).*

It's suggested by some researchers that *Matthew* was originally called *"Levi"*, and it was Jesus who re-named him *"Matthew"* after he was selected as an Apostle.

(St.) Matthew is considered by some scholars to be the author of the first Gospel. However, many researchers believe the writings were not his but the work of an unknown Christian author.

As for Matthew's missionary travels, opinion is likewise conflicting. Eusebius claimed he went to Ethiopia, while others say; Parthia, Syria, Persia, and Macedonia.

Some early historians claim Matthew died of natural causes. According to later researchers, however,

he is believed to have been martyred by the Sanhedrin, or burned to death by cannibals.

Jude's brother Matthew is the patron saint of tax
collectors, and bankers.   He is shown with a spear,
thought to be the object of his martyrdom, and with
wings depicting his role as a missionary.

His feast date is Sept 21, except in the Eastern
Orthodox Byzantine Rite, which is Nov 16.

JAMES THE LESS (Hebrew Jacobi), was perhaps
called *"the Less"* because he was younger, or shorter
in stature than the Apostle, James the Great.

In Scripture, Jude's brother James was a man of
many titles, and was described in several ways:

> *James the son of Alpheus; James the son of
> Mary of Cleophas (Clopas); James, brother of
> Joseph (Joses); James the brother of Jude; the
> Apostle James; James the Righteous One;
> James the Just; James the Younger; author of
> the Epistle of St. James.*

Some Protestant denominations believe James
was the younger brother of Jesus.   This theory is
based on the letter of Paul to the Galatians, and on a
passage in a chapter by Mark:

> *"...but I did not see any of the other apostles,
> except James, the Lord's brother..." (Gal 1:19).*
> *"...Is not This the carpenter, the Son of Mary,
> the Brother of James and Joseph and Judas
> and Simon?   Do not His sisters live here near
> us?..." (Mk 6:3).*

According to Catholic doctrine, the Biblical phrase *"brother of the Lord"* refers to cousins, and relatives.

> *In Hebrew, "brother" was commonly used when referring to relatives. Sister, was the accepted term for the women followers of Jesus.*
>
> *Therefore, "brother", "sister", or "brethren" was used in the broad sense. Furthermore, popular opinion among Biblical scholars, based on several reliable passages in the New Testament, is that Mary did not have any other children.*

Historian Hegesippus wrote that James the Less was a peaceful man who upheld a close relationship with Judaism.

While first Bishop of Jerusalem, his observance of Judaic customs, and ceremonies made him popular among the Jewish people who called him *"the Righteous One"*.

The Roman Catholic Church considers all of the following passages referring to the same person:

> *"..James the son of Alphaeus.."* (Mt 10:3, Mk 3:18, and Lk 6:15)
>
> *"..and his brethren; James and Joseph and Simon and Judas? And do not his sisters, all of them, live near us?.."* (Mt 13:55)
>
> *"..and afterward by more than five hundred of the brethren at once...Then He was seen by James, then by all the apostles.."* (I Cor 15:7)
>
> *"..(Peter) said to James and the rest of the brethren.."* (Acts 12:17).
>
> *"..to see James; all the presbyters had gathered.."* (Acts 12:19).

"...Mary the mother of James the Less and of Joseph.." (Mk 15:40).

"...Mary the mother of James and Joseph.." (Mt 17:56).

"..Jude, a servant of Jesus Christ, and brother of James.." (Jude 1:1)

Traditionally *James the Less* is considered the author of the Epistle of James. However, a number of Biblical scholars believe the letter was the work of an unknown Greek Christian who lived in Antioch in the early 2nd century.

According to *Eusebius' history,* in A.D. 62, the Sanhedrin, ordered James' execution which was carried out by a small group of his own people. (Hist. Eccl. ii. 23:1-19).

The Eastern Orthodox Churches see James the Less and James the son of Alphaeus as separate persons. That is why his feast date is celebrated alone on Oct 9.

The Roman Catholic Church combines the feast date of St. James the Less with St. Philip on May 3. The Anglican feast date for both saints is May 1.

SYMEON (Simeon, Simon). According to the elogium of the Roman Martyrology, Symeon was the eldest of Jude's brothers, about eight years old at the time of Jesus' birth. *(Acta Sanctorum, February, vol. iii, and Hist. Eccl., bk iii).*

He was among the 120 chosen disciples in the Upper Room when the Holy Spirit came on the day of Pentecost.

Symeon was unanimously chosen to succeed his brother, *James the Less,* as the second *Bishop of Jerusalem.* St. Epiphanius, and the historian Eusebius recorded how the Church under Symeon's leadership flourished.

When *Roman Emperor Domitian* ordered the arrest of all of the *race of David,* Symeon managed to evade capture. However, later during Roman Emperor Trajan's persecution of the Christians, Symeon was arrested for being of the *House of David,* and a Christian leader.

He was a very old man when brought before *Roman Governor Atticus.* He was judged guilty, and tortured, before being crucified.

As *Atticus* watched, Symeon endured the pain with courage, evoking great admiration for the aged Christian.

Some historians have tried to identify Symeon with the Apostle Simon the Zealot, but any such connection is extremely weak. (Mt 10.4; Mk 3:18; Lk 6:15; Acts I:13). His feast date is Feb 18.

JOSES (Joseph) was one of Jesus' brethren of whom very little is known. He was referred to by both Mark and Mathew:

> *"...Mary the mother of James and Joseph (Joses)..." (Mt 27:56).*
> *"...brother of James and Joseph (Joses), and Judas (Jude), and Simon (Symeon)..." (Mk 6:3).*
> *"...Mary the mother of James the less, and of Joseph (Joses)...." (Mk 15:40).*
> *"...Mary, the mother of Joseph (Joses), saw where he had been laid..." (Mk 15:47).*

APPENDIX B

INTERCESSORY AUTHORITY

The relationship between departed saints, and the living has been a controversial matter for centuries. Except for *the Anglican community*, certain *Lutheran groups*, and some of *the more traditional Christian denominations*, most *Protestants* do not recognize the intercessory authority of saints.

There are several reasons for this disbelief, the most prominent being the absence of Biblical references about deceased saints. This void is greatly responsible for the misunderstanding.

When the authors of *the New Testament* were recording the early events of Christianity, sanctus *(saint)* was used to describe the *living* faithful follower of Jesus.

(St.) Paul, in his letters to the Colossians (1:2 and 4); and to the Philippians (1:1), leaves no question as to who saints were:

> *"..to the saints at Colossae, our brethren who believe in Jesus Christ..*

> *"..we are told of your faith in Jesus Christ, and the love which you have shown to all the saints.."*

> *"..to all the saints in Christ Jesus that are at Philippi, with their pastors.."*

During the early ages of Christianity, holy persons we know as the saints were then honored as *"martyrs"*.

Children were named after the *martyrs* on whose anniversary they were born, or baptized.

In the third century, two of the most popular names were, *Peter and Paul*.

It was not uncommon for early Christians to travel to the tombs, or places of execution of favorite martyrs where they prayed for intercessory help.

Eventually the definition of *"saint"* changed meaning from a "living" faithful follower of Jesus, to "a *martyr*".

The Apostles, and a number of disciples were among the list of saints.

An interesting note is the original definition of "saint" has been revived by a few modern religions including, The Church of Jesus Christ of Latter-Day Saints (Mormons) who currently use the title "saint" in the Biblical sense to identify active church members.

By the mid-700's the honoring of patron saints had become so widespread, the second *Christian Church Council of Nicaea (A.D. 787)* found it necessary to define devotional status:

LATRIA (Adoration) the highest degree of worship reserved for Jesus, or God.
DULIA (Veneration, Devotion) for saints, and angels as friends of Jesus, or God.
In the late Middle Ages another definition was added: *HYPERDULIA (Highest form of Devotion signifying Special Worship given to St. Mary)*.

In 1563, *the Roman Catholic Council of Trent* defined the respect due to the saints. The council of the Western Church, from which emerged the modern Roman Catholic Church, approved prayers through the saints:

> *"...It is a good and useful thing to invoke the saints on account of the benefits to be obtained from God through their intercession..."*

Religious scholars agree that *prayer is a mystery* because nobody knows exactly how it works. Yet, when discussing the intercessory prayer of saints, many people, including a number of Roman Catholics, are openly skeptical.

A percentage further believe it's a misplacement of faith to focus attention on the saints instead of directly on Jesus. In support of this belief, Paul's letter to Timothy is often quoted:

> *"...there is only one God, and only one mediator between God and men, Jesus, who is a man, like them..."* (I Tim 2:1-8).

Those favoring this passage are not altogether wrong, or for that matter altogether correct. However, when discussing *intercessory prayer of saints,* semantics is perhaps the greatest sinner.

Although grammatically incorrect, it has become acceptable for devotees of patron saints to say such phrases as: *"I pray 'to' St. Jude."* What believers mean to say is:

> *"I pray through St. Jude and other saints, to Jesus who intercedes in my behalf."*

Most devotees of patron saints recognize Jesus as the unique mediating authority between themselves, and the Lord.

Along those same lines, people of average intelligence understand and recognize that it's right and proper to pray directly to God.

But, it's not improper to ask saints for help through their prayers. As for proof of saintly intercessory authority, Jesus made it clear at *the Last Supper* when He told the Apostles about their status after joining Him:

> "...*In My kingdom, you shall sit on twelve thrones, judging the twelve tribes of Israel...*" *(Lk 22:31)*

Jesus told Peter how He had used *intercessory prayer* for him. He further explained that after being reunited with Him in heaven, Peter would be required to *be a mediator for the living:*

> "...*I have prayed for you, that your faith may not fail; when, after a while, you have come back to Me, it is for you to be the support of your brethren...*" *(Lk 22:32)*.

Saint Jerome, who translated the Bible into Latin was convinced of a supernatural earthly-heavenly bond. He wrote that it's right to ask the Angels, and saints for help in obtaining favors from God:

> "...*If the Apostles, and martyrs while alive could pray for others, how much more their power after being united with Jesus in heaven...*"

It must be pointed out that with the exception of *St. Mary*, St. Jude is the most popular of all the saints. He is credited with being the patron saint of:

the Desperate * the Impossible * the Helper of the Hopeless * Desperate and Hopeless Causes * Hopeless and Desperate Cases * Difficult or Hopeless Cases * Lost Causes.

To missionaries who preach under unfavorable, sometimes hostile conditions, St. Jude is the:

"Patron Saint of Difficult Missionary Assignments."

Regardless of what St. Jude is known for, to his countless devotees, he's a friend, guardian, and protector who's always ready to offer comfort, through his intercessory authority.

APPENDIX C

EPISTLE OF ST. JUDE

Among the Scriptural writings is a short, one chapter letter of 25 verses *(Epistle - book - formal letter)* which is credited to *St. Jude Thaddeus, the brother of James.*

Where the letter was written or its intended destination are not known, except the author addressed his message to those familiar with the Bible and Judaic tradition.

In the *New Testament,* this letter is the next-to-the last, coming directly after all the other Epistles, and before the Book of Revelation.

It has been established that when the author learned about the disagreement, and false teachings which had penetrated deep into Christian communities, he wrote an appeal to the faithful to hold their position against the sinful intruders.

Historians reading between the lines, believe the writer was concerned about the materialism, paganism, and shocking immorality of the self seeking Gnostics who believed that knowledge which came through spiritual insight, was the key to life, and salvation rather than faith or works available to all people. The letter was an attempt to harmonize Greek, and Oriental paganism with Christianity, and Judaism.

Many researchers agree that the *"Epistle of St. Jude"* was not written by Jude Thaddeus, but rather an unknown author, perhaps one of his disciples.

Other modern biblical scholars claim there are good reasons to believe the Epistle could not have been written by any Apostle:

From the language used in *verse 17,* it must be concluded that when the Epistle was written, John was the only surviving Apostle.

The author refers indirectly to predictions made by the Apostles as something that happened in the past. He also seems to suggest that he did not considered himself as one of the Twelve.

The date of the composition is unknown, but some scholars believe the period of the writing was between *A.D. 75 and 100.* Politically and socially, conditions point to the years around A.D. 90.

As to the identification of the author of the Epistle, Biblical scholars are divided into two camps:

One separates Jude, the brother of James who wrote the letter, from Jude the Apostle. Those favoring this theory claim the Jude who authored the Epistle is not mentioned anywhere in the New Testament.

Since there's no evidence supporting the conclusion there were two Jude's, the opposition suggests that like some of the other letters attributed to Apostles, Jude's letter was actually written after his death by one of his faithful personal disciples who wished to keep his teachings alive.

A few theologians caution against establishing too late a date on the writing, being too quick to question its authenticity, and eliminating Jude Thaddeus as the author.

Nonetheless, the following is a modern translation of the "Epistle of St. Jude" in letter form:

. . . .

*(1)*Jude, servant of Jesus Christ
and brother of James
(date unknown)

To those who have been called by God,
who have found love in the Father and
have been kept safe by Jesus Christ,
(2) may mercy, peace, and love be
yours and grow in greater measure.

(3) My dear friends:

I've been planning to write to you about the salvation we share. But, now I'm forced to send you this letter of caution. You have a battle to fight for the faith which was handed down and entrusted to the saints.

(4) Godless people, who you had been warned about through the Scriptures, have secretly worked their way into your group. They are corrupting the gifts that our God has given to us and turning them into immorality. These people even deny that Jesus Christ is our one Lord and Master.

(5) Even though you've heard it before, allow me to remind you, how the Lord rescued His people from Egypt, but afterward destroyed those who proved to be unfaithful.

(6) There were also angels who had supreme authority, but didn't keep it and left their heavenly home to mingle with earthly beings. These the Lord

has kept in darkness and in spiritual bondage to be judged on the final day.

(7) Just as the angels did, the people of Sodom, Gomorrah, and the other nearby towns practiced fornication and unnatural vice. Their punishment is a warning to us that they are paying for their sins in eternal fire.

(8) In a similar way, the Godless visionaries among you are doing the same thing. They are polluting their bodies, disregarding authority and slandering the glorious angels.

(9) Even when Michael the archangel was engaged in an argument with the devil over Moses' body, he didn't charge him with blasphemy or use abusive language, but merely said, "May the Lord reprimand you."

(10) These unholy people attack what they do not understand. On the other hand, like unreasoning animals, they are corrupted through the things they instinctively know, which in turn brings about their fatal destruction.

(11) The intruders rush to make the same mistakes as the prophet Balaam, who for reward led the Israelites into sin with foreigners and caused them to sacrifice to idols. Also they're similar to Korah who rebelled against legitimate authority and assumed rights that were not his to take. The Godless will get what they deserve and will share the same fate as the others.

(12) These people are dangerous obstacles to your Christian banquets. They join your solemn religious feasts without shame, but only look after themselves. They are like clouds blown around by the wind that bring no rain. Like barren trees in the fall, they bear no fruit and being uprooted in the winter, they're twice dead.

(13) Godless people are like wild ocean waves, splashing their shameless deeds around like foam, or like shooting stars bound for an eternity of black darkness.

(14) It was with them in mind that Enoch, the seventh generation from Adam, made his prophecy, "..The Lord will come with His countless Holy ones about Him..

(15) "God will pass judgment on all mankind, convict the godless for every evil deed and wicked thing they have done, and sentence those irreligious sinners for every harsh word they have spoken against Him."

(16) These people are grumblers and complainers who live by their passions, governed only by their own desires for boastful talk. To take advantage they resort to flattery.

(17) Remember my dear friends, what the Apostles of our Lord Jesus Christ repeatedly told you to expect:

(18) "...In the final days there will be impostors who will sneer at religion and live by their godless passions and led by their lustful acts."

(19) These sensual people are not with the Spirit and are causing divisions among you.

(20) But you my dear friends, must grow strong in your *faith, praying in the Holy Spirit.*

(21) Keep yourselves in God's love and wait for the mercy of our Lord Jesus Christ to give you eternal life.

(22) Correct those who are confused with doubt and reassure them.

(23) You must rescue those worthy of being saved by pulling them out the fire. But, there are others to whom you must be kind with great

caution, keeping your distance even from outside clothing which is contaminated by vice.

(24) Glory to Him who can protect you from a fall and bring you safe, innocent and happy to His glorious presence.

(25) To the only God who saved us through Jesus Christ our Lord, belongs glory, majesty, dominion, authority and power, which He had from ages past, and now for ages to come. Amen.

APPENDIX D

SHRINES AND OTHER ADDRESSES

St. Jude Mass Leagues are devotional organizations sponsored by the St. Jude Shrines as a way of formerly bringing together the devotees of St. Jude Thaddeus, Apostle.

The intentions of registered League members are remembered in a specified number of Masses, as well as regular, perpetual, and/or Solemn Novenas conducted at the enrolled shrine.

Most Mass Leagues will remember the intentions of members at the offering of daily, and/or weekly Masses on the Altar above the tomb of St. Jude in the Vatican Basilica of St. Peter's.

St. Jude Mass Leagues are the ultimate in *intercessory prayer*, for groups of volunteers gather together in spiritual association to offer the Holy Sacrifice of the Mass for the intentions of registered league members; alive and deceased.

Plenary Indulgences, under the usual conditions, may be gained by members of St. Jude Leagues. For example:

On the day of enrollment.
On the feasts of Christmas, Easter, Christ the King, and St. Jude's feast day, October 28.
On the feast date of the founder of the order of the priests who are charged with the shrine.
On the feast date of the Saint in whose church the shrine may be housed.
At the hour of the members death.

189

Names, addresses, telephone numbers and miscellaneous related information about several of the official St. Jude shrines as well as Mass Leagues and other important addresses are provided below:

NATIONAL SHRINE OF ST. JUDE within Our Lady of Guadalupe Church, 3208 East, 91st St., So. Chicago, Illinois, 60606.

Entrusted to - the Claretian Fathers and Brothers.

St. Jude Mass League, 221 West Madison St., Chicago, Illinois, 60606 - Telephone: 313 236-7782 .
. . . .

SHRINE OF SAINT JUDE THADDEUS within St. Pius Church, 1909 South Ashland Ave., Chicago, Illinois 60608.

Entrusted to - the Dominican Fathers.

No information concerning an active Mass League - Telephone: 312 226-0074
. . . .

THE INTERNATIONAL SHRINE OF ST. JUDE within Our Lady of Guadalupe Church (the oldest church building in the city - Mortuary Chapel of St. Anthony of Padua), 411 North Rampart St., New Orleans, Louisiana, 70112.

Entrusted to - the Missionary Oblates of Mary Immaculate.

League of St. Jude, address same as above.
Telephone: 504 525-1551.

<u>*SHRINE OF SAINT JUDE THADDEUS*</u> (legal title "Shrine of St. Jude Subsidiary of the Province of the Holy Name") within St. Dominic Church, 2390 Bush St., San Francisco, California, 94115.

Entrusted to - the Dominican Fathers of the Province of the Holy Name.

Mass and Novena League, address same as above. Telephone: (415) 931-5919.
. . . .

<u>*SHRINE OF SAINT JUDE*</u> within St. Stephen of Hungary Church, 414 East, 82nd St., New York City, New York, 10028.

Entrusted to - the Franciscan Friars.

Address all petitions and letters to St. Stephen's Franciscan Friary, address same as above. Telephone: 212 -736-8500.
. . . .

<u>*ST. JUDE SHRINE*</u> within St. John the Baptist Roman Catholic Church, 500 West Saratoga St., (Paca and Saratoga Sts.), Baltimore, Maryland 21201

Entrusted to - the Pallottine Priests and Brothers.

League of St. Jude, Promotional Center, 309 North Paca St., Baltimore, Maryland 21201 -
Telephone: 301 685-3063.

. . . .

NATIONAL SHRINE OF ST. JUDE, (Sanctuaire De Saint Jude), 3980 rue St-Denis, Montreal, Quebec. H2W 2M3.

Entrusted to - the Dominican Fathers and Brothers (Les Peres Dominicains).

St. Jude Society and Rosary Center, address same as above Telephone: 514 845-0285.

. . . .

ROSARY SHRINE OF ST. JUDE. within St. Dominic's Church, 4844 Trumbull Ave., Detroit, MI, 48208

Entrusted to - the Dominican Fathers

For further information contact Brother Gerard Thayer OP at the above address of telephone 313 831-7566

. . . .

SHRINE OF ST. JUDE, within the Sacred Heart Church, 183 Bayview Ave., Jersey City, N.J. 07305-3398

Entrusted to - the Dominican Fathers

For further information write to the above address of telephone 201-332-3073

. . . .

CITY OF ST. JUDE, (Legal title: The City of St. Jude, Inc. a corporation created by and existing under the laws of the state of Alabama), 2048 West Fairview Ave., Montgomery, Alabama 36196-9989

St. Jude's Mass League, address same as above. Telephone: 205 265-6791.

. . . .

ST. JUDE CHILDREN'S RESEARCH HOSPITAL, 332 North Lauderdale (P.0. Box 318), Memphis Tennessee 38101 Telephone 901 522-0300

Contributions, bequests and legacies write to: AL-SAC-St. Jude Children's Research Hospital, 505 N. Parkway, P.0. Box 3704, Memphis, Tennessee 38103 or contact your local chapter. Donations Telephone: 901 522-9733.

. . . .

ST. JUDE RANCH FOR CHILDREN has been established to care for children, who, through broken marriages, neglect, mental and physical cruelty, and abandonment find themselves without a home and the love each child so desperately needs.

Many of the children who arrive at St. Jude's are spiritually, morally and mentaly broken. They've been abused battered, neglected and understandably filled with anger, hatred, despair and confusion. Some of the children openly admit a desire to take their own young lives.

The typical child admitted to St. Jude's has marked difficulties in school resulting from the turmoil experienced in his or her short lifetime.

One hundred percent of all contributions made to St. Judes Ranch goes directly to the support of the children.

For information, telephone Father Herbert A. Ward Jr., *702 293-3131* or write to: St. Judes Ranch for

Children, 100 St. Jude's St., P.O.Box 985, Boulder City, Nevada, 89005-0985

. . . .

LEAVES *(from the Garden of St. Bernard)*, established in 1938, is a bi-monthly magazine published by the Mariannhill Missionary Fathers of the American Province.

The Congregation of Mariannhill Missionaries (C.M.M.) is a pontifical mission society of priests and brothers conducting extensive missions in South Africa, Zimbabwe (Rhodesia) and New Guinea, as well as mission establishments in the U.S.A., Canada, Brazil, Holland, Spain, Germany, Italy, Switzerland, and Austria.

Subscribers to Leaves are kept on the mailing list as long as they indicate they wish to receive the magazine. Since the cost of publication is defrayed by the goodwill offerings of its large readership, there is no regular subscription rate. For further information write to:

Leaves, P.0 Box 87, Dearborn, Michigan, 48121-0087
Telephone: 313 561-2330.

Mariannhill Mass League was established by Pope Pius X on October 6, 1906, and has been blessed and recommended to the faithful by successive popes.

On Sept. 22, 1984, Pope John Paul II recommended membership when he wrote: *"...Convinced that the Mariannhill Mass League can contribute to the spread of Christ's name..."* For particulars concerning the Mariannhill Mass League write to the above address.

Mr. Spencer wants to congratulate all who are responsible for the publication of Leaves: the Editor-in-Chief, Rev. Anthony Kirschner, C.M.M.; the Managing Editor, Rev. Timothy Mock, C.M.M.; the Editor, John P. Gillese; and the associates and contributors who have made Leaves a magazine of outstanding excellence.

Since every edition of the bi-monthly publication is filled with articles and stories of an inspirational and informative quality, Mr. Spencer saw the Mariannhill magazine as an important source of research material.

Throughout *"Thank You Saint Jude,"* reference is often made to published stories, quotes, and articles supporting devotion to St. Jude, and the power of intercessory prayer through the saints.

APPENDIX E

HIS NOVENAS NEVER FAIL

In Christian usage, a *novena* is a devotion consisting of the repetitious reciting of a set form of prayers over nine consecutive periods such as; *nine successive days, or a certain day within nine consecutive weeks.*

A novena may be made at any time, and repeated at will. In an emergency novena prayers may be recited on nine consecutive hours within the same day.

The novena has a long history dating back to Ascension Thursday, when the Apostles, and 120 disciples:

"...went back to Jerusalem... into the Upper Room where they stayed...with one mind, gave themselves up to prayer, together with Mary the Mother of Jesus, and the rest of the women and His brethren..."

"...When the day of Pentecost (Sunday, nine days later) came round, while they were all gathered together in unity of purpose...they were filled with the Holy Spirit, and began to speak in strange languages..." (Acts 1:12-14 and 2:1-5).

During the *early Middle Ages*, novena prayers patterned after the action of the Apostles, and disciples became associated with the saints.

The faithful who were in need of help turned to their patron saints through the novena. Small groups with a personal devotion to a particular saint began gathering for nine days of prayer.

In 1675, Jesus appeared in a vision to *(St.)* Margaret Mary Alacoque, a French Visitation nun, and recommended the use of the novena. *(She was canonized in 1920)*.

> *Jesus asked Sister Alacoque to dedicate her life to the encouragement of a special novena feast in honor of the Sacred Heart.*
>
> *The novena should begin on the Friday after the octave of Corpus Christi (The Thursday following Trinity Sunday - earliest May 17, latest June 20), and be repeated every first Friday for nine successive months.*
>
> *Jesus promised all who receive Holy Communion throughout the nine month novena would be given help to remain in the state of sanctifying grace until death (final perseverance). Also, the Sacrament of "Anointing the sick" would be administered before death (formerly Extreme Unction)..*

In the nearly two thousand years since the very first novena in the Upper Room, only four basic forms have developed:

> *MOURNING THE DEPARTED* through a novena of Masses. This novena of ancient origin is perhaps the oldest form of public novena. Although created for the departed, it's rarely used.
>
> *PREPARATION FOR SPECIAL OCCASIONS.* During the early Middle Ages this novena was popular as a preparation for the feast of Christmas.

Later, it evolved into a nine month novena of Masses in honor of the length of time St. Mary carried Jesus in her womb.   It then spread from Spain to other countries, and by the 17th century was commonly celebrated.

PRAYER TO THE SAINTS.   Until the 1600s this novena was made for the recovery of health.   Today it is popular with devotees seeking special favors through the intercessory power of patron saints.

INDULGENCES AND SPECIAL GRACES. Not until the 19th century did the Roman Catholic Church formally approve, and recommend this form of novena.   Currently, this novena form is continued by those seeking Graces, and Indulgences.

Today, novenas in honor of St. Jude, and other saints are made both publicly, and privately:

Devotees of the *"Patron Saint of Hopeless and Desperate Cases"* who make private novenas, do so in their homes, while jogging, when tied up in heavy city rush hour traffic, etc.

Others make private novenas in combination with nine successive daily Masses, or on the same day for nine consecutive weeks, (i.e. nine Tuesdays).   As a rule, those favoring this method mentally recite St. Jude novena prayers in the solitude of the church following Mass.

Where neighborhood churches offer regular weekly, or monthly public St. Jude novenas, the number of devotees taking part is impressive.

The ultimate in this form of public devotion is the *Solemn St. Jude Novena* which begins in a church of shrine on Oct. 20th; concluding nine days later on St. Jude's feast day, Oct. 28th.

St. Jude's reputation of always answering those who make novenas in his honor is widely recognized.

Yet, in the Jan-Feb '84 edition of *"Leaves,"* a disappointed person wrote about making a novena to the "Patron Saint of the Desperate," and not receiving an answer:

"...Your novena to St. Jude, which is said 'never to fail,' can fail. I'm proof!..."

A reply, published in the Jul-Aug '84 edition of the same magazine came from a Mary H. D. of Lynn, Massachusetts.

"My dear father brought up five children on the sight of one eye, as he had an accident at the age of 12, playing rugby in Ireland.

"When he was in his 80's, he was chopping wood when a splinter lodged in his good eye, causing him to become completely blind.

"After many weeks in the Massachusetts General Hospital in Boston, he was released as incurable.

"Furthermore, his doctor said that he had a blood clot behind the eye. If the splinter didn't remain locked in place, he was in danger.

"If it moved too fast it could travel to his brain and he would probably die. On the other hand, if it moved slowly, it would eventually reach his heart and kill him.

"Every morning and every night, one of us would put a drop of St. Jude oil in his eye and recite the St. Jude prayer."

Like Holy Water, St. Jude Oil is considered sacred. It is pure oil of olives blessed with a relic of St. Jude and believed to restore health of body, and mind.

"We did this faithfully, non-stop! Suddenly in the 8th month my father's sight miraculously returned.

"The first thing he saw was the colors on my dear mother's apron. When I got home from work, my Mom told me that Pa wanted to see me in the dining room.

"As I entered, he looked up and said: 'Don't move, I always want to remember you as you are now.'

"My father lived until he was almost 89 and all that time, enjoyed his new found sight."

St. Jude's record of coming to the aid of those who faithfully pray for his help is documented in millions of *letters of testimony* received at the various shrines.

Yet, there are people, like the person who wrote to "Leaves," who believe their petitions had been rejected.

To help these people understand what should be expected from a novena, the pastor of the Immaculate Conception church in West Springfield, Massachusetts, Father Timothy Hallahan explained:

"I've been conducting regular weekly novena services in honor of St. Jude for nearly nine years.

"During that time, I've witnessed the intercessory power of the "Saint of the Impossible" many times over.

"One fact I'm sure of is that novena prayers through St. Jude may be answered in months or years, and not always according to human schedule.

"It's important to understand that God doesn't have to comply to our rhythm of things.

"St. Jude novena services have been held at my church for the last 50 years, yet, I've never met a person who has complained about attending novenas for any period of time, and not having had their prayers answered."

LETTERS OF TESTIMONY

"I have been devoted to St. Jude for over 30 years. My powerful patron has helped me in so many ways, so many times. He has pulled me through, and helped me more times than I can count...D.Y., Sioux City, Iowa."

"Thank you St. Jude for helping my daughter get the teaching she desperately wanted, and needed...B.G., Ship Bottom, N.J."

About eight years ago my son gave up his religion, and was into drugs and alcohol. Some months ago I started the novena to St. Jude, and soon my son began asking different questions about religion.

Next, he went to confession, and for the first time received communion... W.F., Stratford, CT."

"A lump on my breast was diagnosed as cancer. I prayed to St. Jude, and two days later the cancer disappeared. My doctor cannot explain what happened. M.O."

"I was arrested on charges of murder and arson. I asserted that I was innocent, but my trial ended with a verdict of guilty. I was sentenced to six to 12 years in prison. I maintained I was innocent, and still do.

"I had never heard of St. Jude until my mother sent me a booklet about him. I started to ask him for help, and while my innocence has not been acknowledged, my sentence has been reduced to three years with less time perhaps for good behavior. I feel St. Jude helped me, and will in time help me prove that I am, and was innocent..."

"My daughter was married for seven years, and the doctors gave no hope for her having a child. I continued to pray to St. Jude for her. I want to thank God, through St. Jude's intercession, I now have a beautiful grandson...C.H., Carmichael, Calif."

"Some 46 years ago my sister left home and disappeared. Our family prayed, and asked St. Jude to have her found, or at least to contact us. On New Year's day our prayers were answered; she phoned...G.F."

"I was faced with a grave and apparently hopeless situation. I asked the intercesssion of St. Jude and after that a series of extraordinary

coincidence took place in which there was an answer to my prayers. Thank God that we have someone to depend upon under such circumstances."

"I prayed for over six years, and through the intercession of the Blessed Mother, St. Jude, St. Benedict, and St. Gerard my son has recovered from drug and alcohol abuse, and my daughter, suffering the same affliction, has taken the first steps toward recovery...K.M.M.

"Last winter I had surgery on the roof of my mouth. Complications set in, and I lost some of the tissue resulting in a hole in the top of my mouth. The doctors told me they were sure nothing could be done except to be fitted with a retainer so that I would be able to eat and talk.

"Then I remembered how St. Jude had helped my father once. I started to pray to him, and before long a kind of peace came over me. By spring the hole in my mouth had completely closed. The orthodontist who was called in to make my retainer told me that what happened is medical history..."

"I am writing in thanksgiving to St. Jude, for interceding for my son who had spinal meningitis. He was given up for dead, but I continued to pray to St. Jude. My baby is now healthy...I.A., Tampa, Fla."

"I was operated on for 'carcinoma of the prostate.' I prayed through St. Jude for help. Some 16 months later, I was operated on again, and the same doctor told me he couldn't understand what had happened for the diagnosis was benign. I wish to thank St. Jude for what I consider a miracle...J.B. Sun City, AZ."

"A dear friend is a diabetic who recently went into shock. He lives alone, but managed to telephone us for help. We live 75 miles away, so by the time we arrived, he was unconscious and his right foot and leg had turned black.

At the hospital, the doctor said the leg would have to be amputated at the knee. I petitioned St. Jude, and by morning we were informed that only his foot would have to be removed. Two days later, they said only two toes would have to be amputated. With the help of St. Jude my friend is leading a fairly normal life with two legs, two feet, and ten toes...M.V.A."

Many people who are accustomed to making St. Jude novenas do not realized that a combination of factors are necessary for petitions to be granted:

Perseverance when all seems hopeless.
A working partnership.
A sincere relationship with St. Jude.
Unconditional faith in his intercessory ability.

Jesus left no room for debate when He stated that anything can be accomplished with a combination of faith and prayer.

"...I promise you, if you have faith and do not hesitate, you will be able to do more than I have done..."
"...If you say to this mountain, remove and be cast into the sea, it will come about. If you will only believe, every gift you ask for in you prayers will be granted..." (Mt 21:21-22).

Apparently, Jesus also wanted it understood that in addition to faith and prayer the element of "a working partnership" was desirable.

For instance there's the story of Jesus and the blind man:

> *"...Jesus spread clay on the blind man's eyes, and said to him, 'Away with you, and wash in the pool of siloe' (meaning, sent out). So he went, and washed there and came back with his sight restored...." (Jn (:1-8).*

Certainly, Jesus had the power to give sight to the man on the spot. Apparently, He used this particular incident to send out the message:

> *"God helps those who help themselves."*

Later in the 4th or early 5th century, St. Augustine wrote that God will answer prayers, but only in partnership with those willing to help themselves. About this he wrote:

> *"...Work as if everything depends on you; pray as if everything depends on God..."*

All of St. Jude's living friends didn't learn about him through prayer cards, or newspaper ads, but always knew of his special intercessory power through family devotion.

However, because they had experienced few valleys during their lives, the need to seek his aid had not been felt.

Suddenly they're confronted with a life threatening situation, and the familiar cry for St. Jude's help goes out. Such is the story of Army Private, Jerome S. Becker:

> *"I wouldn't be alive today if it were not for St. Jude. It happened during WW II when I was with the Third Infantry Division in Europe.*
>
> *"One day during fierce fighting, I was hit four times; in the face, legs, and back. For six long days and nights I lay on the battlefield alone, without any help.*
>
> *"When I thought I had been abandoned, I began to despair. Suddenly, out of the nowhere I thought about St. Jude.*
>
> *"In the middle of the 'no man's land,' I cried out: 'St. Jude, help me!' At that very moment a voice answered, 'Where are you?' It was a rescue squad. I spent 8 months in various hospitals recovering from my wounds.*
>
> *"Later I entered the Dominican Order and was ordained in 1953. I have never forgotten how my prayer for help was instantly answered."*

Today, as a missionary priest, Father Becker conducts novenas in honor of his patron saint. Every so often, as part of a sermon, he'll tell the story of how St. Jude answered him.

Before closing this section, it's important to correct a misconceived notion concerning novena prayers.

In today's world, there is a substantial number of educated people of faith who are afraid to make St. Jude novenas. Moreover, they will not allow others to pray in their behalf.

These people have the distorted belief that whenever a patron saint helps to get prayers answered, something treasured is taken away, or the problem is replaced by a different one.

Such unfounded fears are innocently spread by warning others about the dangers of novena prayers. The real mystery is how such superstitions begin.

. . . .

To devotees familiar with St. Jude Thaddeus' novenas, the following suggested prayers may be helpful.

For those not accustomed to this form of devotion, but would like to make a novena in honor of the "Patron Saint of Desperate Cases," the suggested format, and prayers are offered.

APPENDIX F

ST. JUDE NOVENA PRAYERS

In the Name of the Father, and of the Son, and of the Holy Spirit. Amen

. . . .

Pallottine Priests and Brothers
St. Jude Shrine - Baltimore, Maryland

O glorious Apostle, St. Jude Thaddeaus, true relative of Jesus and Mary, I salute you through the Most Sacred Heart of Jesus! Through this Heart I praise and thank God for all the graces He has bestowed upon you.

Humbly prostrate before you, I implore you through this Heart to look down upon me with compassion.

Oh, despise not my poor prayer; let not my trust be confounded! To you God has granted the privilege of aiding mankind in the most desperate cases.

Oh, come to my aid, that I may praise the mercies of God. All my life I will be grateful to you and will be your faithful client until I can thank you in heaven. Amen.

. . . .

NOVENA PRAYER - FIRST DAY

Dominican Fathers
National Shrine of St. Jude - Montreal, Canada

0 dear St. Jude, my help and protector, you know the real motive of my novena. In this hour of need, I lay at your feet my trials and numerous difficulties.

Do not forsake me, you who had the privilege of being closely related to Jesus, a constant companion in His childhood, and later one of the Twelve Apostles, collaborating daily with Him to spread the good news of the Gospel, and by doing so, bringing souls closer to His Divine Heart.

By some mysterious dispensation of Divine Providence, you were one of the least known of the Apostles. You had been neglected and forgotten. Do not forget me in this hour of need and, through your intercession, may my prayers be answered. Amen.

. . . .

NOVENA PRAYER - SECOND DAY

Dominican Fathers
National Shrine of St. Jude - Montreal, Canada

0 glorious Apostle St. Jude, Patron of Desperate Cases, after the Ascension of Our Lord, you brought into the far distant countries the Gospel of His Redemption.

To the King of Edessa, you gave the consolation and comfort of faith and trust in Jesus, the Son of God.

Finally, your lengthy apostolate of word and example was crowned by your heroic martyrdom.

I beg you to come to my help by your merits and sufferings accepted in union with and for the love of your Divine Master; intercede for me at the throne of God and grant me, with the shortest possible delay, the favor I so fervently demand. Amen.

. . . .

NOVENA PRAYER - THIRD DAY

Dominican Fathers
National Shrine of St. Jude - Montreal, Canada

0 good St. Jude, we Christians, heirs of your teachings and your merits, have for many centuries almost forgotten you.

We beg you to pardon us for having too long allowed your name to be confused with that of Judas Iscariot who sold his Master for thirty pieces of silver.

We now honor you as the ever faithful Apostle, remembering at all times your special grace of fidelity to the Divine call.

Being ever a constant, gentle, faithful friend of Our Lord, you have safeguarded this intense bond of friendship with becoming modesty.

Prevailing upon your friendship and loyalty, I beg you today to be my intercessor with God and to ask Him to grant me the favor I implore in all confidence and humility. Amen.

. . . .

NOVENA PRAYER - FOURTH DAY

Dominican Fathers
National Shrine of St. Jude - Montreal, Canada

0 glorious Apostle, St. Jude, you were a witness to the many miracles performed by our Divine Savior.

You saw Him restore the sight to the blind, hearing to the deaf and health to the sick.

You were there when He brought back to life the widow's son.

With the other Apostles, you were in the boat when our Lord heard your desperate cries and you saw, at His command, the angry waters become calm again.

Jesus performed these miracles that you might believe in His Divinity.

You, whom we have called the Saint of the Impossible, implore of your Divine Master the request I fervently ask, and by obtaining for me this special favor, increase my faith in Our Lord and also the trust I have in you. Amen.

. . . .

NOVENA PRAYER - FIFTH DAY

Franciscan Fathers
Shrine of St. Jude - New York City, N.Y.

0 Forgotten Saint! Deep was the anguish that overwhelmed you during the Passion of your beloved Master!

You saw Him lavish His love and His gifts on mankind; you saw Him give sight to the blind, heal the lame and raise the dead to life.

And when the selfish cruelty of men raised Him on the Cross of Suffering, and then laid Him away from you in the tomb, your anguish knew no bounds.

By the bitter sorrow which you experienced then, have pity on me now, in my hour of trial.

Come to my assistance and ask your beloved Master to grant me the grace and consolation I seek in this bitter moment.   Amen.

. . . .

NOVENA PRAYER - SIXTH DAY

Franciscan Fathers
Shrine of St. Jude - New York City, N.Y.

O inspired saint! To you it was given to receive the Third Person of the Blessed Trinity, the Holy Spirit, under the visible form of a Fiery Tongue.

You know what it meant to hide in fear and trembling from the wrath of men, until the Holy Spirit came with His gifts.

Obtain for me those same gifts, that under the inspiration of God the Holy Spirit, I may understand God's will in my particular trial, that I may act prudently in all things, and that I may persevere in the service of God despite trials, temptations and persecutions.   Amen.

. . . .

NOVENA PRAYER - SEVENTH DAY

Franciscan Fathers
Shrine of St. Jude - New York City, N.Y.

0 zealous Apostle! Having received from Christ, your Master, the commission to teach all nations, you spread the doctrines of your Divine Cousin far and wide.

No distance was too great; no labor too difficult; no persecution too strong to keep you from the fulfillment of your vocation.

You taught not by word alone, but also by your example. 0 beloved Apostle! Intercede for me that I too, by cooperating with God's Grace, may be able to bring the knowledge and love of God into the lives of others by my words and my manner of living. Amen.

. . . .

NOVENA PRAYER - EIGHTH DAY

Dominican Fathers
National Shrine of St. Jude - Montreal, Canada

Glorious St. Jude, during your life, in silence and humility, you accomplished with unswerving fidelity your daily work.

Obtain for me the grace to understand that the sure means of gaining your special protection is my faithful performance of my daily work in union with Jesus, and for Jesus.

Grant that I may live as a perfect Christian, inspired by a determined courage in the least details of my ordinary life, so that even my small actions may be performed, to the best of my ability, for the love of God, thus helping me to acquire your virtues.

By this means, I am confident that I will draw down upon me always your sustaining aid and your most powerful protection. Amen.

. . . .

NOVENA PRAYER - NINTH DAY

Dominican Fathers
National Shrine of St. Jude - Montreal, Canada

The One that exalts the humble wills now that your power be acknowledged and your merits be acclaimed by all.

Already, in all parts of the world, your influence with God is known, invoked, and proclaimed.

At your request, humble St. Jude, Our Redeemer, the Savior and Supreme Judge of our souls, bestows His most precious favors on those who go to Him, through you.

This is the reason that persuades me today to have recourse to you.

Following your example, I will understand that Divine favors will be granted me inasmuch as I strive to know myself better, to realize how much I need God, to remain obedient, faithful, and truly humble. Amen.

. . . .

PRAYER TO ST. JUDE

Claretian Fathers -
National Shrine of St. Jude, Chicago

Most holy Apostle, St. Jude, faithful servant and friend of Jesus, the Church honors and invokes you universally, as the patron of hopeless cases, of things almost despaired of. Pray for me, I am so helpless and alone. Make use I implore you, of that particular privilege given to you, to bring visible and speedy help where help is almost despaired of.

Come to my assistance in this great need that I may receive the consolation and help of heaven in all my necessities, tribulations, and sufferings, particularly (Pause here and make your request) and that I may praise God with you and all the elect forever.

I promise, 0 blessed St. Jude, to be ever mindful of this great favor, to always honor you as my special and powerful patron, and to gratefully encourage devotion to you. Amen.

. . . .

This prayer to St. Jude may be recited when problems arise, when you seems to be deprived of all visible help, or for cases almost despaired of.

. . . .

SPECIAL PRAYER OF
PRAISE AND THANKSGIVING

Franciscan Friars - Shrine of St. Jude - N.Y.

0 most sweet Lord Jesus Christ, in union with the unspeakable heavenly praise with which the Most Holy Trinity glorifies itself, and which thereafter flows upon Your Sacred humanity, upon Mary, upon all the angels and saints, I praise, glorify and bless You for all the graces and privileges You have bestowed upon Your chosen Apostle and intimate friend, Jude Thaddeus.

I pray You, for the sake of his merits, grant me Your grace, and through his intercession come to my aid in all my needs, but especially at the hour of my death, strengthen me. St. Jude, model of humility, mirror of patience, lily of chastity, flame of divine love, intercede for us! St. Jude, comforter of the sorrowing, refuge of sinners, helper of the distressed, special patron in hopeless cases, intercede for me! Amen.

. . . .

SPECIAL PRAYERS FOR A HAPPY DEATH

Dominican Fathers the Province of the Holy Name
Shrine of Saint Jude Thaddeus -
San Francisco, California

Oh, my Lord and Savior, support me in that hour in the strong arms of Your Sacraments, and by the fresh fragrance of Your consolations.

Let the absolving words be said over me, and the Holy Oil sign and seal me, and Your Own Body be my food, and Your Blood my sprinkling;

And let my sweet Mother Mary breathe on me, and my Angel whisper peace to me, and my glorious Saints, St. Jude and *(name's of other patron saints)* smile upon me; that in them all and through them all, I may receive the gift of perseverance, and die, as I desire to live, in Your faith, in Your church, in Your service, and in Your love. Amen.

- Cardinal Newman

. . . .

May He support us all the day long, till the shades lengthen, and the evening comes, and the busy world is hushed, and the fever of life is over, and our work is done!

Then in His mercy may He give us a safe lodging, and a Holy rest, and peace at the last! Amen.

- Cardinal Newman

. . . .

SPECIAL PRAYER AT
THE DEATH OF A LOVED ONE

*Dominican Fathers the Province of
the Holy Name Shrine of Saint Jude Thaddeus -
San Francisco, California*

St. Jude, you know the loneliness of my heart since God took *(name of deceased)* to *(his-her)* eternal reward.

Make me realize taking *(name of deceased)* from me was not for my harm, but that I might look for *(name of deceased)* always in your presence. Amen.

. . . .

SPECIAL PRAYER FOR MENTAL ILLNESS

*Dominican Fathers Province of
the Holy Name Shrine of Saint Jude Thaddeus -
San Francisco, California*

Compassionate St. Jude, you have restored health and soundness of mind to so many through the Power of God, see me *(or name of afflicted person)*, in this suffering.

Confident of your powerful intercession, I beg you to ask Jesus, the merciful Healer of the sick, to restore me *(or name of afflicted person)* that helped by His love I (or name of afflicted person) may experience once more that great gift of mental health. Amen.

. . . .

SPECIAL PRAYER FOR DRUG OR ALCOHOL ADDICTION

*Dominican Fathers the Province of
the Holy Name Shrine of Saint Jude Thaddeus -
San Francisco, California*

Dear St. Jude, *drug/alcohol* addiction has caused a terrible upset in my family.

The victim of this self-inflicted sickness has lost all sense of true reality, the reality of love, as well as, the reality of life.

Beg Almighty God to make this addict aware that true euphoria can only be found in heaven and not with chemical dependence. Amen.

. . . .

SPECIAL PRAYER FOR AN ALCOHOLIC

*Dominican Fathers the Province of
the Holy Name Shrine of Saint Jude Thaddeus -
San Francisco, California*

St. Jude help me in this sickness which is spiritual, psychological, and physical.

Strengthen my weak faith, no matter what may befall me. Teach me to be patient and serene in the midst of troubles.

St. Jude, help me so that nothing will upset me or weaken my determination to stay sober and abstain from alcoholic drink. Amen.

. . . .

SPECIAL PRAYER IN MARITAL DIFFICULTY

*Dominican Fathers the Province of
the Holy Name Shrine of Saint Jude Thaddeus -
San Francisco, California*

St. Jude, we have problems with our marriage. Beg Almighty God to give us the light to see ourselves and each other as we really are.

Help us to grow daily in self-knowledge and mutual love, while at the same time developing our potential to love and be loved.

Help us, St. Jude, to see and root out every manifestation of selfishness and childish self seeking, those hidden enemies of love and maturity.

Thus learning to love and being filled with love, we may complement each other the remaining days of married life. Amen.

. . . .

SPECIAL PRAYER FOR WORK

*Franciscan (Friars)
Shrine of Saint Jude - New York City, N.Y.*

0, Son of God and Son of the Virgin Mary, Thy Sacred Heart is an ocean of mercy, compassion and love for all men, but especially for the poor.

To Thee I come, filled with confidence, to place my prayer for work in Thy Sacred Heart.

Thou didst come to preach the Gospel to the poor; Thou didst consecrate poverty by choosing it for Thine own life.

0, Sacred Heart of Jesus, hear my prayer for work and in Thy Mother's name grant my request. Amen.

. . . .

SPECIAL PRAYER FOR THE PHYSICALLY ILL

*Dominican Fathers Province of
the Holy Name Shrine of Saint Jude Thaddeus -
San Francisco, California*

St. Jude, I have not the strength to pray as I should. Nothing is able to give me any relief.

My courage is faltering, impatience and loneliness are clouding my mind and my heart.

Obtain for me, St. Jude, the courage, and resignation to accept all these trials from the hand of God with faith and patience.

If it is for the good of my soul, grant that I may recover my former health so that I may be of assistance to others. Amen.

. . . .

SPECIAL PRAYER FOR THE PHYSICALLY OR MENTALLY ILL

*Missionary Oblates of Mary Immaculate
International Shrine of St. Jude -
New Orleans, Louisiana*

Consider, Oh Lord, Your faithful ones, suffering from bodily and mental affliction, and refresh the lives which You have created, that by being bettered by suffering, they may ever be conscious of Your merciful salvation.

May the Lord, Jesus Christ, be with me, to guard me; within me, to preserve me; before me, to lead me; behind me, to watch me; above me, to bless me.

Who lives and reigns with the Father in the Holy Spirit in Eternity. Amen.

CONCLUSION TO NOVENA PRAYERS

LORD'S PRAYER

(Recite three times)

Our Father, who art in heaven, hallowed by Thy name; Thy kingdom come; Thy will be done on earth as it is in heaven.
Give us this day our daily bread and forgive us our trespasses, as we forgive those who trespass against us; and lead us not into temptation, but deliver us from evil. Amen.

. . . .

HAIL MARY

(Recite three times)

Hail Mary, full of grace! the Lord is with thee; blessed art thou among women, and blessed is the fruit of thy womb, Jesus.

Holy Mary Mother of God, pray for us sinners, now and at the hour of our death. Amen.

GLORY BE

Glory be to the Father, and to the Son, and to the Holy Spirit. As it was in the beginning, is now, and ever shall be world without end. Amen.

. . . .

St. Jude, pray for us.
St. Jude, graciously hear us.

. . . .

In the Name of the Father, and the Son, and of the Holy Spirit. Amen.

. . . .

SHORT NOVENA PRAYER

The following prayer may be recited as a complete novena. It's suggested that the prayer conclude with an Our Father, Hail Mary, and Glory Be.

. . . .

(Claretian Fathers - National Shrine of St. Jude, Chicago)

St. Jude Thaddeus, relative to Jesus Christ, glorious Apostle and martyr, renowned for your virtues and miracles, faithful and prompt intercessor of all who honor you and trust in you! You are a powerful patron and helper in great affliction.

I entreat you from the depths of my heart; come to my aid with your powerful intercession, for you have received from God the privilege to assist with your visible help those who almost despair of all hope. Look down upon me.

Time and again I find myself discouraged and depressed by the troubles I must face. I know that others around me have burdens as heavy or heavier than mine, but I sometimes come close to despairing that I will not be able to continue carrying mine.

Overwhelmed by these thoughts, I ask your help. *(pause to make your request).* Do not forsake me in my sadness. Hasten to my aid. I will be grateful to you all my life and will honor you as my special patron. I will thank God for the graces bestowed upon you, and will encourage honor to you to the best of my ability. Amen.

. . . .

HYMN TO SAINT JUDE

Apostle of Jesus, a martyr-saint of old;
The cousin of Our Savior, of Whom thy love hath told.
A writer of the Scriptures, with tongues of fire aflame;
The worker great of wonders, in Jesus' Holy Name.
The worker great of wonders, in Jesus' Holy Name.

St. Jude, tho oft forgotten, thou shall remembered be;
We hail thee now in glory, and have recourse to thee.
For hope for the despairing, when hopeless seems the task.
And from the Heart of Jesus, through thee we favors ask. And from the Heart of Jesus, through thee we favors ask.

BIBLIOGRAPHY AND COMMENTARY

This bibliography and commentary includes references cited within the text of this work. References quoted in complete form have not been duplicated here.

<u>HEGESIPPUS</u> was a Judeo-Christian and native of Palestine who lived about the middle of the 2nd century.

He was a well-informed traveler, collector of Christian tradition, Church historian, and an author of five books of Memoirs which survive only in fragments.

What's left of the collection of his works have nearly all been preserved within *the Ecclesiastic History of Eusebius.* Portions of *(St.)* Hegesipppus' books, believed to have existed in some libraries as late as the 16th and 17th centuries, dealt with the early Church at Jerusalem.

Even though Hegesippus' stories have a legendary quality, most researchers agree the material has important biographical value, since it is not limited to the New Testament narratives.

<u>EUSEBIUS </u>of Caesarea, *(260?-340?),* theologian, scholar, and Church historian, was considered to have been one of the most learned men of his time.

About *A.D. 314,* he became Bishop Eusebuis *(Pamphili)* of Caesarea, a seaport of ancient Palestine, about 30 miles north of Joppa (Tel Aviv-Yafo).

Eusebuis was a productive writer who published a *"History of the World until 303,"* and a *"History of the Christian Church through 324."* (His. Ecc. 2.40).

His history (IV, xxxii, 1-3) led the to conclusion that *(St.)* Hegesippus apparently recorded a succession-list of the early Bishops of the Church.

If the published material is authentic, the list represents the earliest witness of the names of the first Roman Bishops.

Eusebuis also wrote a detailed account concerning the *Apostle, Jude Thaddeus, and the healing of Prince Abgar of Edessa.*

The ancient historian claimed authentication for his work came from documents he discovered in the *Archives of Edessa* of which he personally translated from Syriac into Greek.

It must be pointed out that some scholars believe the manuscripts in question were forgeries. However, in all fairness, a greater number of historians consider Eusebius the *"Father of Church History,"* and believe he was an honest, and careful researcher, and a scholarly writer.

TEN BOOKS OF CRATON: Craton was a dedicated *disciple of Jude Thaddeus.* During the final 13 years of the missionary lives of Jude and Simon the Zealot, Craton traveled with the pair of Apostles; faithfully keeping a diary of all that happened.

APOSTOLIC HISTORY OF ABDIAS (Historia Certaminis Apostolici) consists of ten books describing the lives, travels, activities, works, and martyrdoms of several of the Apostles.

Abdias translated the *Ten Books of Craton,* into Hebrew, and incorporated the diary material into Book VI of his ten books of history.

Book VI.1-6 concerns the missionary life of Jude Thaddeus, and Simon the Zealot while in the Parthian Empire.

Even though Abdias was not a biblical writer, and the material used in his history was drawn from a mixture of sources, *(legend, folklore, and other stories passed down through the ages)*, his books have often been quoted.

For centuries Book VI has been widely accepted as an authentic account of the 13 year missionary partnership of *Jude and Simon.*

In later years, Abdias' history was translated from Hebrew into Greek by his disciple, *Eutropius.* In the 3rd century, the history compiled by Abdias was once again translated, this time from Greek into Latin by *Julius Africanus,* a close friend of *philosopher, Origen (185-254).*

Origen was an ambitious writer who is said to have authored some 6000 religious books.

ST. JEROME *(340-420),* the best of the early interpreters of the New Testament, translated Abdias' history into Latin. He also quoted other source material in the *"Ecclesiastical History of Rufinus",* and his Latin translation of the *"Recognitiones"* of Clement.

As a matter of interest, it was St. Jerome who, upon completing an intensive study of the Scriptures, as well as the *"Apostolic Constitution",* confirmed that Jude Thaddeus *(Lebbeus)* is the same man who preached in Edessa.

The *"Homily on Matthew"* (10:4) by St. Jerome is another excellent source of research material.

JAMES OF VORAGINE *(1228-1298)* Dominican friar, Archbishop of Geneo, and author of *"The Golden Legend,"* was another prominent theologian who had relied on Abdias' collection.

Other early esslesiastical writers, and historians who often borrowed from Abdias' ten volumes are: *Scholasticus Evagrius; St. Ephrem the Deacon,* who died in Edessa in *373;* and *St. John Damascene (676-758).*

ACTS OF THADDAEUS is a fascinating set of Edessene legends beginning with the exchange of letters between Jesus, and Prince Abgar of Edessa. The Greek document identifies Addai as Thaddaeus *(Labbaeus)* one of the Apostles.

TEACHING OF ADDAI, is a Syriac document written during the 5th century. Many scholars believe that Addai's material appears to be the earliest written report of the missionary adventures of Jude Thaddeus.

ST. ADDAI (Jude Thaddeus) has been honored as the evangelist who brought the words of Jesus into the towns, and cities around the Tigris and Euphrates.

Although there's little solid historical evidence concerning the foundation of the Catholic Church in these communities, there's no question that Christianity was introduced into this region at a very early date.

Reliable ancient records provide testimony that as long ago as the late 2nd century, the king of Edessa, *Abgar IX (179-214)* was a Christian.

Also, during the same era, *(A.D. 190 to 203),* the disciple *Palouth* served as the Bishop of Antioch.

Even today, the Catholic Chaldeans, the Nestorians of Iraq, and the Kurds of Kurdistan, refer to St. Addai *(Jude Thaddeus)* as the *"Holy Apostle".*

The people believe St. Addai was the founder of their church, and the author of their liturgy.

GOSPELS (Greek, *auangelion - Latin, evangelium,* "*good news or tidings*") is a valuable source of research material for archeologists, and historians of religion.

The English word *"Gospel"* is derived from the Middle English "godspel" which meant *"good tale"*, but later came to mean *"God's Story."*

The first three books *(Gospels)* of the new Testament are believed to have been written by Matthew, Mark, and Luke at various times between *A.D. 65 to 80.*

These books are known as the *"synoptic gospels"*, for they contain similar accounts, and give a summary, or synopsis of Jesus' life, teachings, and His earthly Galilean ministry.

The Gospel of John is the fourth book, believed written about *A.D. 90.* It contains an account of Jesus' life in Judea, as well as many events not recorded in the first three Gospels.

None of the Gospels provide a complete story of the life of Jesus. Each is a collection of oral, and written accounts of His acts, and words.

The Acts of the Apostles is the fifth book of the New Testament. It is believed to have been written by Luke, a close companion of Paul, some time before *A.D. 80.*

This book records the thirty year history from the establishment of the Christian Church beginning with the Ascension of Jesus.

It also contains many of the works of the Apostles, and disciples, ending with the second year of imprisonment, and removal to Rome of the Evangelist *(St.)* Paul.

/

In conclusion, is a listing of prominent historians, theologians, and saints whose works contributed to this biography of St. Jude Thaddeus.

For various reasons, however, proper identification, or credit has not been given within the body of the text. Their names are:

ST. POPE CORNELIUS *(r.251-253)* who was banished by Roman emperor Gallus, and martyred in 253.

ST. CYRIL, Bishop of Jerusalem *(315-387)* whose writings are a valuable source of history.

ST. AMBROSE (340-397), Bishop of Milan, one of the four doctors of the Western Christian Church.

ST. CYRIL, Bishop of Alexandria *(376-444)*, one of the early Fathers of the Church.

ST. ISIDORE (Latin, Isidorus Hispalensis) *(560-636)*, a Spanish religious leader, encyclopaedist, and Bishop of Seville, Spain.

ST. BEDE (Baeda) *(673-735)*, an English theologian who modern scholars consider the most intelligent historian of the early Middle Ages.

ST. NICEPHORUS *(758-829)*, a Byzantine-Roman, and patriarch of Constantinople.

MARTYROLOGISTS: anonymous researchers who studied the history of the lives of martyrs. Their work provided invaluable details concerning the death of Jude Thaddeus.

ABOUT THE AUTHOR

John Wallace Spencer is a man of many talents and diversified interests which have contributed richly to his career as a broadcaster, investigative reporter, writer and lecturer.

He is a published author of several international best-seller books including the 2 1/2 million copy runaway hit: Limbo of the Lost, (*the first work written exclusively about the notorious Bermuda Triangle. This book remained on the New York Times' Best Seller List for eleven weeks)*; Limbo of the Lost-Today, *(updated accounts about the mysterious triangle zone)*; No Earthly Explanation; The UFO Yearbook; For Fun and Profit, and Thank You Saint Jude.

Publication rights to several of Mr. Spencer's books were purchased by foreign publishers. Corgi Publishing distributed three of his books throughout Great Britain. Other international firms translated Mr. Spencer's works for sale in Germany, France, Spain and Japan.

Mr. Spencer's most recent work, *Thank You Saint Jude* is unquestionably his most important, for it is the only book exclusively devoted to the *Patron Saint of the Desperate*. In fact, it is the only written, in-depth study about the wondrous rediscovery and miraculous current popularity of the once forgotten Apostle.

Thank You Saint Jude has been sanctioned as theologically sound. After careful study Spencer's manuscript was granted an *imprimatur* from the Most Reverend Joseph F. Maquire, D.D., Bishop of the Diocese of Springfield, Massachusetts, and a *nihil obstat* from Passionist missionary Father Augustine Hennessy, C.P., former editor of Sign Magazine.

For thirty years, Mr. Spencer has worked in every phase of the commercial radio and television broadcasting industry including: announcer, talk show conversation host, program and news director, and vice president-general manager of his own radio station. He has worked as a newspaper reporter, editor, salesman, teacher, actor, investigative reporter, author, lecturer, and public affairs representative.

From 1952 to 1962, during the Korean and Vietnam wars, the author served on active duty with the U.S. Air Force. After receiving his honorable discharge, Mr. Spencer was appointed Official Investigator for the renowned *National Investigations Committee on Aerial Phenomena (NICAP)*, headquartered in Washington D.C. Throughout the mid-60/70s, he was recognized as one of the nation's top ten authorities on unidentified flying objects.

During the mid-70s, he was placed under contract to Universal Motion Picture Studios in Hollywood, California. Later, he became a regular cast member of a professional New York City repertory company and appeared in a number of long running stage plays.

As an author, Mr. Spencer has been an invited guest on many of the top network and syndicated radio and television conversation programs hosted by such noted celebrities as:

Burt Reynolds *(NBC-TV Tonight Show)*; Dick Cavett *(ABC-TV)*; Tom Snyder *(NBC-TV Tomorrow Show)*; Dave Garroway; Betty Furness; Joyce Davidson *(CBC-TV)*; David Susskind; Mike Douglas; Vidal Sassoon; Mike Connors *(ABC-TV Wide World of Entertainment)*; Lucy Arnaz; Regis Philbin; Bill Bogg (Midday Live); Garry Moore *(To Tell the Truth)*; Bill Cullen *(NBC Monitor)*; and many others.

He has also been interviewed by a legion of local radio and television talk show hosts and newspaper reporters from coast to coast. On several occasions his publishers sent him on promotional book tours to the major United States and Canadian cities.

As a professional public speaker, for more than two decades, Mr. Spencer has been appearing before university, college, and club audiences. While presenting fascinating re-creations of events, he draws out the human side of his subjects.

The author attributes his longevity as a sought after radio and television talk show guest and professional lecturer to the philosophy of the famous 1950s television network personality, the late Bishop Fulton J. Sheen who taught that; *"young and old alike are tantalized by once upon a time, particularly when the stories are about real people."*

Mr. Spencer is currently President of the Phillips Publishing Company, a firm he founded in 1969. He is also a professional television broadcaster, commercial announcer, an active member of the U.S. Air Force Reserve, and an FAA licensed multi-engine rated airplane pilot.

The author has traveled extensively throughout the United States, Canada and Europe. He has resided in New York, Massachusetts, Mississippi, Tennessee, New Jersey, Connecticut, Iowa, Great Britain and Germany.

INDEX

237

238

239

240

242

243